KNOW THE MIDDLE EAST JOHN LAFFIN

GW00385313

ALAN SUTTON
1985

Alan Sutton Publishing Limited
Brunswick Road · Gloucester

First published 1985

Copyright © John Laffin 1985

British Library Cataloguing in Publication Data

Laffin, John
  Know the Middle East.
  1. Near East
  I. Title
  956'.052   DS44

  ISBN 0-86299-215-X

Typesetting and origination by
Alan Sutton Publishing Limited.
Printed in Great Britain
by The Guernsey Press Company Limited,
Guernsey, Channel Islands.

AUTHOR'S NOTE

This book describes many of the problems and pitfalls of the Middle East which await the foreign businessman, traveller, writer and politician, and the ordinary tourist. It deals with aspects of political, commercial, social, family and personal life not found in text books or travel books, but so essential to an understanding of Middle Eastern peoples. An Arab proverb says, 'Caution does not advert the decree of fate.' In view of what this says about Middle Eastern life, an English language proverb, 'Forewarned is fore-armed', is better advice for all those people who do not come from the Middle East. *Know the Middle East* is, in fact, a survival aid.

The book is not merely the result of my experience alone – though this is wide. The various entries have been read by Arabs of several races, by Turks, Iranians, Israelis and Cypriots. Many of the comments are quoted from distinguished Arab scholars and writers, such as Sania Hamady, Fawaz Turki, Majid Khadduri and Albert Hourani. Every entry has been 'approved' by a second person, generally an expert in the particular field. Country entries – such as that for Algeria, Iran, Turkey and Israel – have been read by nationals of those countries.

Unlike some other books about the Middle East this one is not partisan; it simply seeks to tell the truth about matters which affect foreigners. A multitude of terms and definitions has been used to describe the 'Middle East'. No general agreement exists as to its boundaries but in Western experience and in popular understanding the Middle East comprises almost the entire Arab world as well as Iran, Sudan, Turkey, Israel and Cyprus. This is the area which I regard as the Middle East.

Fascinating and frustrating, always complex and sometimes cruel, this region is like the human navel – the core of the world. And through its pipeline umbilicus flows the oil which sustains the world. Whatever happens here sends shockwaves everywhere. The 'Middle East' has an hypnotic fascination for the mass media, for statesmen and for the public. It can be a fatal fascination and over the centuries many nations have been lured to these hard, hot lands by visions of wealth and empire, only to be destroyed or seriously damaged – the Romans, Greeks, Ottomans, British, Italians, French, Germans, Americans, Russians. Now the 'Western world' is urgently trying to understand the Middle East and its people. This book will help inform the people of other races of the many difficulties which lie in wait for the inexperienced.

Although this is more a book of observation than opinion, where opinions and judgments are expressed – other than those attributed to particular people – they are mine.

JOHN LAFFIN

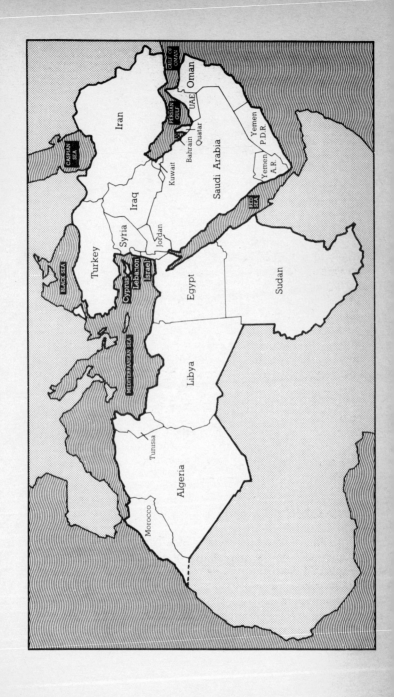

KNOW THE MIDDLE EAST

ALAWITES

Members of one of the smaller, more extreme sects of Islam, the Alawites are also known as the Alawis and earlier they were the Nusayris. They are a sub-sect of the Shi'a Muslims and are strongest in Syria; while making up only 10 per cent of the population they are nevertheless the ruling group. President Hafez Al-Assad is an Alawite. As a minority the Alawites suffered greatly under Sunni Muslim rule but gradually became strong in the army officer corps. These officers brought General Salah Jedid to power in 1966. Within the Alawite sect are individual tribal and family rivalries which go back centuries and the strongest clan in 1970 produced Assad as president. All key posts have been held by Assad Alawites ever since and the country has been stable, by Arab terms, but at great cost; to preserve their control the Alawites have killed their more dangerous Sunni and other opponents.

See ASSAD: SYRIA: ISLAM: TRIBES: MASSACRES

ALCOHOL

Alcoholic drink is forbidden to Muslims, who make up the greater part of the population of the Middle East. The Prophet Muhammad first forbade his followers to use wine before coming to prayers lest they should not understand what he was saying; at a later stage came total prohibition.

The prohibition is largely based on Chapter 2 of the Holy Koran which states: 'In them (wine and gambling) is great sin, and some profit . . ., but the sin is greater than the profit.' Nevertheless, in other Chapters, notably 47, 'rivers of wine' are available in paradise. This may be partly responsible for the ambivalent attitude of many Arabs to alcohol; they shun it in the Middle East but freely imbibe when they visit foreign cities. In many countries, notably Saudi Arabia and Iran, the ban on strong drink is enforced and transgressors may be severely punished. Westerners resident in these countries may drink alcohol but only in private and they must not offer it to local people. Foreigners who 'incite' Muslims to drink have been imprisoned and flogged.

In Israel alcohol is freely available but Israelis are abstemious people and drunkenness is rare. Alcohol is totally prohibited in their armed forces and even in service messes only water or soft drinks are available. Visitors to Israeli homes would not necessarily offend by taking a present of spirits or wine but it is wise to make some inquiries about the family's attitude to alcohol. Middle East Christians drink alcohol but rarely in public, even when dining out in a good restaurant.

See ISLAM: KORAN: RAMADAN

ALGERIA

Modern Algeria dates from July 3, 1962 when the country, after a notoriously savage war against France, won its independence. In terms of Middle East politics Algeria is regarded as a hardline state; that is, it wants the total destruction of Israel. It has only one political party, the Liberation National Front, although parliamentary elections of a kind were held in March 1982. From 1979 President Chadli has achieved significant changes in the structure of government and in economic policy. There is continuing debate over the direction and pace of economic development while Islamic resurgence and the desire of younger people to maintain a pragmatic socialist outlook present pressing challenges to the administration. Non-alignment is the fundamental of foreign policy although

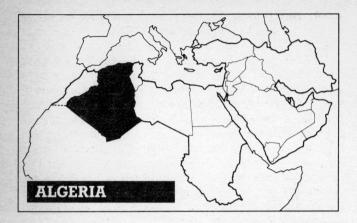

ALGERIA

Algeria leans towards the West, particularly in regard to economic matters.

A meeting between Heads of States of Algeria and Morocco in 1983, the first for 10 years, followed by easing of border restrictions, is an indication of better relations. In the same year Algeria and Tunisia signed a friendship treaty.

The country is a curious mixture; while progressive politically, it is retarded socially. Women have few rights and in most regions they are little more than chattels and sex objects. Those women who are educated enough to be aware of their inferior status have emigrated to France. Algeria remains largely French-speaking and its strongest trading links are with France. Islam is a powerful force with Sunnis in the great majority. Most of the 20 million Algerians are of both Arab and Berber stock. Only 60,000 Europeans, mainly French, live in Algeria.

Algeria possesses enormous and varied mineral wealth and exploration of vast areas of the Sahara is expected to yield much more oil and other minerals. Most of the new industries and all heavy industry is state-owned; the private sector controls the textile industry, food-processing and a significant part of the distribution industry.

In 1983 only a third of secondary pupils and a fifth of university students were girls. Students are expected to

spend part of their vacations working and teaching in the
countryside for the good of the nation. Two years of
military service are compulsory for school and university
leavers. National servicemen are used as a cheap general
labour force. Over 54 per cent of Algerians are aged 17 or
less and in the cities large numbers of adolescents are
unemployed.

Many strikes take place but are covered up. Attempts by
the government-controlled trade union federation to
browbeat the strikers by accusing them of 'working for the
imperialists' are sometimes successful. Gross inequalities of
the kind seen in some other developing countries are not
general in Algeria but the highest paid are still 20 times
better off than unskilled workers. Algeria is not overall a
corrupt society but some corruption exists, notably in the
private sector and especially in the marketing of farm
produce and the supply of foodstuffs and building
materials.

The network of state enterprises and co-operative
organisations, which effectively control the importing and
distribution of a wide range of articles, is bureaucratic and
often extremely inefficient. Bureaucracy must increase
because the National Charter guarantees the integration of
'non-exploiting private property' into the social system.

There have been police round-ups to clear the streets of
Algiers and other cities of what are called 'hooligan' and
other 'parasitic elements'. Some of these are probably
Iranian-inspired agitators trying to promote the Islamic
revolution.

ARABS

Of all regions in the world that with the longest recorded
history is occupied by Arabs; chronologically it covers 7,000
years of settled human life, two-thirds of which are recorded
by well-documented written records. The Arab world
covers 5,300,000 square miles, consists of 21 states and at
least 150 million people.

The racial origins of the Arabs are ancient. Cherished
traditions tell of the Flood and of Noah, a survivor of that

catastrophe and the father of the human race. His three sons, Shem, Ham and Japheth were the progenitors, respectively, of the ancient Arabs' three divisions of the world – Arabia, Africa and the rest. The Arab reconstruction of mankind as seen by the desert men 2500 years ago is clearly an inheritance from the Arabs' linguistic cousins and ancient neighbours, the Jews. The son of Shem (from whose name our words 'Semite' and 'Semitic' derive) had two sons, Qahtan and Adnan. Qahtan was the begetter of the Arabs of the south, Adnan of those of the north. Whether this is true or not is irrelevant; what matters is that Arabs accept it.

Many Arabs define an Arab as one who speaks Arabic as his native tongue, though the form of language differs from region to region. There is literary Arabic and colloquial Arabic.

Arabs are concerned with the definition of an Arab in a way that would never occur to people of other races to define themselves. The Lebanese scholar, Clovis Maqsud, has written: 'An Arab is one whose "destiny" is, either by force of circumstance or intentionally, bound to the Arab world as a whole . . . Whoever is descended from Kurdish, Negro or Armenian stock, if he inhabits an Arab country he becomes an Arab by force of circumstances and by free association of his own destiny with that of the Arab world.'[2]

Many Arabs would agree with the international scholar Professor H.A.R. Gibb[3] that, 'All those are Arabs for whom the central fact of history is the mission of Muhammad and the memory of the Arab empire and who in addition cherish the Arabic tongue and its cultural heritage as their common possession.'

An old Arab proverb says a good deal about the Arab people:

'The enemy of my friend
is my enemy;
The enemy of my enemy
is my friend.'

The principle governs much Arab political, economic and

even social activity, even though the Arab race is widely scattered and covers people geographically spread from Morocco in the west to the Persian Gulf in the north-east.

Dr Sania Hamady,[4] herself an Arab and one of the great authorities on Arab psychology, says that to the individual 'Life is a fearful test' for 'modern Arab society is ruthless, stern and pitiless . . . It worships strength and has no compassion for weakness.' Hamady says that Arab social life is 'full of pain, bitterness and insecurity'. She summarises the Arab with compassion and insight: 'Arabs' laziness, lack of perseverance and irresponsibility, their procrastination and lying must be understood to know what to expect of them and how to approach them . . . To the Arab, provided nobody knows, any wrong is permissible . . .'

On the personal level, the Arab, accustomed to emotivity and impulsiveness in his speech, tries to communicate a certain idea to Westerners in ways they cannot comprehend. He shouts, he gets excited, he threatens and rebukes. This is the normal way in which Arabs communicate with each other. Conversely the Arab will interpret Western calmness as lack of responsiveness and sympathy to his ideas. Trying to impress on an audience the fact that he means what he says, the Arab resorts to emphatic assertion and exaggeration.

Anybody dealing with Arabs must understand some significant facts, which I present here without pejorative intent.

To the Arab there may be several truths about one situation, depending on the type of language he is using.

A linguistic truth over-rides a perceptual one; that is, what language can be made to say about a situation has more validity than what the eyes or reason might say. Language is not used to reason but to persuade, but on analysis it can be seen that the greater the rhetoric the lesser the substance. Among Arabs the value of words is often assessed by quantity but at the same time meanings are not constant from one person to another. Language creates violence, justifies and excuses it; indeed, words can justify or rationalise anything. Similarly, literature exists to persuade (as in the Koran) and to delight. It is not designed to stimulate the intellect but to incite the senses.

The Arab means what he says at the moment he is saying it, but five minutes later he may say the exact opposite. He is neither a vicious liar nor, usually, a calculating one; he lies naturally and 'normally'. Westerners must be patient with the Arab in discussion. He does not come directly to the point, hence the lengthy discussions about the buying and selling of, say, a camel; the camel is rarely mentioned until the third day's talking.

Ishaq Musa al-Hussayni,[5] a Palestinian, lists the causes of crisis in Arab thought:

Uncertainty: Because of widespread faith in destiny there is little planning.
Extemporisation: When problems arise suddenly, solutions are improvised and are often wrong.
Absence of reason: There is no process of correct and logical thinking based on study and meditation.
Absence of self-criticism: 'The thinking man among us is suspect . . .' al-Hussayni says.
Obsession with the past: This, al-Hussayni writes, paralyses the Arab mind.

The Westerner involved in negotiations with Arabs needs to begin with certain basic assumptions, and possibly Sania Hamady is the best authority to state them. She stresses that the Arab gives because he expects to receive; that he is tied hand and foot by the demands and interferences of his group; that an Arab becomes enthusiastic and proclaims his readiness to act but when the time comes he shies away, and that he feels debased if he is pitied. Hamady, too, draws attention to the Arab's quick, intense anger. Perhaps, most importantly, no foreigner should assume that because an Arab does not say 'No' that he means 'Yes'.

ARAB LEAGUE _____

With British encouragement, seven nations brought the

Arab League into existence in 1945 – Egypt, Lebanon, Syria, Iraq, Transjordan, Saudi Arabia and Yemen. The principal stated aims at the time were to strengthen ties between the participant states and to produce closer co-operation economically, culturally and in communications. Soon, however, the League's preoccupations became termination of the British mandate over Palestine, an end to Jewish immigration and a drive for 'Palestinian Arab independence'. In 1953 the members signed the Arab League Collective Security Pact but it had little significance, the League failed to achieve its aims because it grew too large – to 22 members including the Palestine Liberation Organisation (PLO). For many years the League's headquarters were in Cairo but when Egypt signed a peace treaty with Israel they were moved to Tunis and Egypt's membership was suspended. The League has little political strength because of the numerous bitter divisions in the Arab world but it has served its purpose as a kind of information exchange.

ARAFAT, Yasser

Born in Gaza on August 23, 1929, Yasser (or Yasir) Arafat's full name is Abd el-Rahman Abd el-Rauf Arafat el-Qudwa el-Husseini. Abd el-Rauf is his father's name, which Arabs customarily add to the full name. Arafat has avoided mentioning his full name for it reveals his kinship to the former Grand Mufti of Jerusalem, Haj Amin el-Husseini, a pro-Nazi who lost his status in the Arab world. As a youth Arafat was involved in street fighting and while living in Jerusalem during the years of World War II he was a member of a gang which brawled with Jews and attacked British shops. During 1949, in Gaza, Arafat led a gang which fought bloody feuds with the Nashashibi tribe.

By 1951 he was an engineering student at Cairo University and in 1953 he joined other students in irregular operations against British troops in the Suez Canal zone. As president of the Palestine Students Federation (1952 – 56) he became connected with the extreme Muslim Brotherhood.

In 1956 he was a junior officer in the Egyptian Army during the Suez Crisis but the following year he fled from Egypt when the Muslim Brotherhood was outlawed. Moving to Kuwait, Arafat became a building contractor. Using the *nom-de-guerre* of Abu Ammar, he toured the Middle East, preaching 'liberation of Palestine' and recruiting members for his organisation, Fatah. In 1965 he began to win control of the refugee camps in Jordan and Lebanon.

In 1967, in the wake of the Arab defeat by the Israelis in the 'Six-Day War', Arafat's Fatah began a campaign of terror against Israel and against Jews everywhere. Surviving several assassination attempts by rival terrorist leaders, Arafat plotted to take over Jordan but with tens of thousands of PLO members he was driven out of that country in 1970 by King Hussein's army.

Arafat became leader of the PLO, which by 1970 was a wealthy organisation, and in 1974 he was permitted to speak to the United Nations General Assembly, even though he wore a revolver on his belt. He has always considered this to be one of his greatest propaganda triumphs. Usually dressed in crumpled khaki and wearing a checked kaffiyah he became increasingly interesting to Arab journalists. They presented him as he wanted to be presented, living an austere life of physical hardship and personal sacrifice. 'I am married to Fatah,' he was often quoted as saying. 'Fatah is my woman, my family, my life.' Arafat is humourless but when with journalists he is often expansive and warm.

After the PLO was defeated by the Israelis in the war of 1982 and forced to withdraw from Beirut, Arafat lost some credibility among his own followers but not in the world at large. Later that year Pope John Paul granted him a private audience, which was the result of several years' patient manoeuvring by the PLO 'Foreign Minister', Farouk Khaddoumi. After intense friction within the PLO, which the Syrians wanted to control, Arafat's authority declined and his life was considered to be in danger. While it is possible that some individual terrorist might kill him, other PLO leaders know that if Arafat were to disappear, ten years would be needed to build up another figurehead with Arafat's connections, influence and popularity. His biographer, Thomas Kiernan, notes that 'By his very nature Arafat is not a statesman . . . he has little understanding of political processes and programmes.' Arafat often says that the world should not forget that the 'Palestinian movement' was born of violence and achieved its greatest recognition as a result of violence.

It is important for Westerners to know that Arafat is more highly regarded outside the Arab world than within. Arab leaders distrust him and suspect him of intriguing against them; at various times he has had serious quarrels with King Hussein, King Khalid and presidents Sadat, Mubarak, Gaddafi, Assad, Nimieri and Hussein of Iraq. For his own ends he has supported Ayatollah Khomeini's 'Islamic Revolution' and he is in turn aided by Khomeini. Most significantly, after his 1982 defeat in Lebanon, a good many ordinary Palestinians no longer see Arafat as their hero and saviour.

See PALESTINE LIBERATION ORGANISATION: LEBANON: TERRORISM

ARMENIANS

See CHRISTIANS

ASSAD, Hafez el-

Born in 1928, Assad is an Alawite by religion and therefore a member of Syria's ruling Alawite minority. After an undistinguished career he became Minister of Defence as well as Commander of the Air Force in February 1966. He seized power in 1970. At the time King Hussein of Jordan was engaged in a 'civil war' against the Palestine resistance movement and Salah Jedid, the president, proposed to send military aid to help the PLO. Assad objected to this, arrested Jedid and assumed national leadership. In February 1971 the Ba'ath Party elected him as president. Fiercely hostile to Israel, he joined President Sadat in a joint Syrian-Egyptian attack against Israel in October 1973 (the

Yom Kippur War). The Syrians lost still more territory to Israel but Assad's skilful handling of the military disengagement talks with the Israelis enhanced his standing in the Arab world.

Assad's regime is based on the Alawite sect's loyalty, on the sympathy of certain minority and 'outside' groups – such as the ruling Saudis – and on the strength of the Ba'ath Party cells in the armed forces and the civil service. His brother, head of the security and secret police, is quick to deal with anything regarded as a threat to the regime. Assad's own appeal to Syrian nationalism above that of region or sect loyalty has weakened the forces which oppose him.

Insistent on gaining control over Lebanon in his ambitions for a 'Great Syria', Assad sent an occupation army into Lebanon during the civil war of 1975–76; it has remained there ever since, at vast expense to his country. He accepts Soviet military and economic assistance and is the principal Soviet ally in the Middle East, but he pursues an independent and almost personal policy. Implacable in his hostility towards Israel, Assad threatened to kill President Sadat personally for his having made peace with Israel. He rarely leaves Syria for fear of a coup taking place in his absence and in 1985 he was by far the longest serving president of Syria. His five predecessors were violently deposed.

See ALAWITES: DICTATORSHIP: SYRIA

ASSASSINS

This was the name given to a murderous group of Syrian Muslims led by a mysterious prophet known as the Old Man of the Mountain. The word 'assassin' first appeared in the chronicles of the Crusades in the 12th century. The writers did not then know that the Old Man had established a remarkable haven for his followers in the fortress and valley of Alamut, which was headquarters of the sect for centuries. He enclosed the valley and turned it into a beautiful garden with many varieties of fruit. Its elegant palaces and pavilions were gilded and the walls were covered with exquisite paintings. Runnels flowed freely with wine and milk and honey and water while women, said to be the most beautiful in the world, played music, sang sweetly and danced seductively. The Old Man wanted his people to believe that this really was paradise, so he fashioned it after the paradise described by Muhammad in the Koran. Here the young Assassins indulged themselves in every pleasure until the Old Man needed their services. Then a young man would be taken to the Old Man. 'From whence came you?' he would ask. 'From Paradise,' was the ritual reply. 'Go then and slay a man I shall name,' the Old Man would command. 'When you return you shall be again in Paradise and should you die, nevertheless my angels will carry you to Paradise.'

Thus manipulated the young Assassin would do whatever his master asked of him. Information about the superlative skill of the Assassins in disguise and murder and of their fanaticism and devotion reached European ears through descriptions of such travellers as Marco Polo and Odoric of Pordenone.

The Assassins belonged to the Isma'ili sect, a dissident group and offshoot of the Shi'a Muslims, whose quarrel with the Sunnis was – and remains – the major schism in Islam. The 'enemy' for the Isma'ilis was the Sunni establishment. Murders of Sunni leaders were designed to frighten, weaken and eventually overthrow Sunni Islam. In a calculated war of terror, the Assassins killed sovereigns, princes, generals, governors and priests who had condemned Isma'ili doctrine. 'To kill these people is more lawful than rainwater,' said one Assassin leader. 'To shed the blood of a heretic is more meritorious than to kill seventy Greek infidels.'

The Assassins had a complex organisation with agents in many towns so that an agent on a mission could travel across Iraq and Syria without the need to meet strangers who might report him to officials. The Assassins have no precedent in the planned, systematic and long-term use of terror as a political weapon. The Assassins flourished for centuries and their services were bought by ruthless leaders. The Muslim Arab terrorist organisations, notably Black September of the PLO, the Abu Nidal group, the Muslim

Brotherhood and the Iranian murder squads who swear allegiance to Ayatollah Khomeini and his mullahs could be considered the modern equivalent of the Assassins. See TERRORISM

ASSASSINATION

Murder as a political act is a long established practice in the Middle East and it does not arouse the horror which it causes in the West. For instance, the assassination of President Anwar Sadat of Egypt in 1981 was accepted throughout the Middle East as an inevitable result of his having signed a peace treaty with Israel – it was a 'natural' consequence of making peace with 'infidels'.

Middle Eastern rulers always run the risk of being killed by opponents. Since 1948 revolution and military take-over, nearly always with bloodshed, has been the most common means of reaching power in the Arab world. Between 1948 and 1983 30 heads of state and heads of government were murdered. The monarchs include King Faisal of Iraq, King Abdullah of Jordan, King Faisal of Saudi Arabia. In all, more than 140 major political murders and innumerable unsuccessful assassination attempts were recorded between 1948 and 1983 and it must be assumed that many cases were not reported.

Nearly every new leader who reaches power in a coup finds it necessary to kill his predecessor in the process in case he should stage a counter-coup. One of the most recent top-level assassinations was that of Bashir Gemayel, president of Lebanon, in 1982.

BAHA'I

The Baha'i faith is a world religion which established its centre in Israel; about 7,000 Baha'is live in Israel and another 20,000 in Iran. Named after its founder, Baha' Allah, ('the Splendour of God') Bahaism developed out of the Babi, a Sufi or Muslim mystical movement, which was founded in 1844 in Persia. It upholds the unity of God, urges its followers to search after truth and preaches promotion of unity and peace among peoples. It maintains equality of rights for men and women, prohibits monasticism, advocates an auxiliary international language and has abolished priesthood. The entire human race is 'one and whole,' Baha'is claim. Members of the faith live in more than 11,000 localities and their spiritual and administrative centre is the Universal House of Justice, erected in 1963 in Haifa. The principal shrine, the great and beautiful mausoleum, Maqam-l A'la, is also in Haifa and was completed in 1953.

Baha'ism was favourably disposed to Zionism, believing that the return of the Jews to Palestine was foretold in the writings of its founder. In June 1948, soon after the establishment of the state of Israel, a Baha'i leader wrote to Prime Minister Ben Gurion expressing 'loyalty and best wishes for the prosperity of the new state,' and recognising the significance of 'the ingathering of the Jews in the cradle of their faith'.

In retrospect perhaps the Baha'is were too honest, for this utterance has been held against them by the more fanatical of Islam's leaders, such as Ayatollah Khomeini. The Khomeini regime regards Baha'is as inferior 'because they favour the Jews' and hundreds have been accused of being spies. Many have been executed. In fact, the ethics of the Baha'i movement make all Baha'is strictly non-political. A major cause for Iranian hatred is that the Baha'is treat women as the equals of men and the members of all religions as equal with one another and because they have no priests.

BAHRAIN

The State of Bahrain comprises a group of 35 islands situated midway along the Persian Gulf and 30 km. off the east coast of Saudi Arabia. Bahrain is the largest island, being 50 km. long with a maximum width of 17 km. The population is only 359,000, 60 per cent of them being Shi'a Muslim, though Bahrain has Christian, Hindu, Baha'i and Parsee communities. Bahrain was under British control

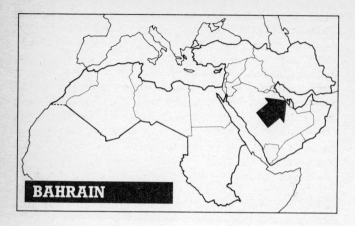

BAHRAIN

after World War II but throughout the 1950s internal politics were affected by the growing nationalist fervour which spread throughout the Arab world after the rise of Nasser in Egypt. Quarrels between the Sunni and Shi'a communities caused acute tension. By the early 1970s Britain's plans to withdraw from 'east of Suez' helped the ruling family, the el-Khalifas, to initiate political reforms. Independence was proclaimed on August 14, 1971.

Experiments with parliamentary democracy have proved unsuccessful and Sheikh Isa rules by decree. But more radical members of the National Assembly have continued to press for the recognition of political parties and an increase in the proportion of elected members. The Khalifa family fears that such moves would further increase sectarianism and factionalism. Very much exposed to the effects of the Iranian revolution from just across the Gulf, Bahrain has to move cautiously in its relations with the West. Iran long ago claimed Bahrain as its own and the Khomeini regime repeatedly renews this claim. In 1981 police foiled an Iranian plot to assassinate Sheik Isa and key members of his government. Since May 1979 Saudi Arabia has promised to ensure Bahrain's independence and is building a 15-mile four-lane causeway to provide the first land link between the two countries. The country is also supported by the other members of the Gulf Co-operation

Council (GCC), Kuwait, Qatar, United Arab Emirates and Oman.

In view of its limited oil reserves Bahrain is putting much effort into diversifying the economy. Being close to important shipping lanes and linked to both western and eastern time zones, it has used its geographic advantages to establish a Major Middle East service centre and has built an industrial base around hydrocarbons, aluminium smelting and ship repair; Bahrain had 12 per cent of the world's ship repair business in 1982.

Since Bahrain began granting licences to offshore banking units (OBUs) – that is, foreign banks – in 1975 the sector has been one of the most successful parts of the diversification strategy; the assets of the more than 143 banks run to over 60,000 million dollars. The OBUs do not pay tax on profits or on depositors' interest income. Bahrain's time-zone is such that its working day overlaps with those of all the world's major financial centres. They open their doors at 7 a.m. to handle traffic from Tokyo and do not shut their doors until 12 hours later, to catch the New York money markets.

Bahrain is one of the most 'relaxed' of Arab states; Sheikh Isa permits alcohol and Bahrain's supper clubs offer the best in gulf entertainment. Already many Saudis fly to the island looking for fun and members of the austere Saudi royal family fear that Bahrain will turn into a gigantic weekend resort when the causeway road is open in 1985. Bahrain allows the US Navy to use its ports regularly and has good relations with Washington.

BARGAINING

The first price asked or offered in any dealing in Middle Eastern countries, excluding Israel and to some extent Cyprus, is not to be taken seriously. This principle applies from a petty purchase in a bazaar to a major operation in international trade. Middle Eastern people get great pleasure from the process of buying and selling and many are keenly disappointed when a prospective partner in a deal simply agrees to the terms without demur. This rarely happens among the natives of a country who will haggle over a few cents and question the price of something which a Westerner would regard as too trivial to bother about. Of course, there are exceptions. The price of an airline ticket is what the desk clerk says it is and haggling over the cost of a room at any one of the Hilton hotels in the Middle East would be considered outrageous. But in general the prices of goods and services can be 'discussed'. C.S. Coon[6] says: 'The merchant sits in his shop reading a book or chatting with the neighbour in the next booth. The customer appears and asks the price of a pair of slippers. Merchant and customer may argue over this for half an hour. Friends and bypassers join in the sport. The customer pretends to go away, the merchant to put back his goods. Finally the customer buys the slippers, usually at a reasonable price. Why, asks the foreign visitor, do they go to all this trouble? Why not just tag the merchandise with a fixed price? Because the merchant likes to bargain with his customers. It is his job and he enjoys it. From his point of view it is not a waste of time. Some day he will get a gullible customer and make a killing. But that is less important than the pleasure this kind of inter-action gives him.'

Sometimes the shopkeeper or the customer interrupts the bargaining by introducing some irrelevant topic, then the haggling is continued. In some sections of Middle Eastern society a deal is discussed vehemently and noisily and a stranger could easily imagine that buyer and seller are quarrelling in a rage. But the apparent anger is normal and expected. Again, a shopkeeper will often say when asked the price of an article, 'Receive it as a present.' This answer is a common form of speech and the seller knows that the prospective buyer will not take advantage of it. The ritual is for the buyer to ask the price again – and the seller will now ask an exhorbitant price.

Sania Hamady[4] says that the trading ritual is an illustration of the ways Arabs complicate situations and ideas far beyond their real difficulty. 'They imagine every task to be so difficult as to be incapable of being achieved except the hard way.'

Westerners often make the mistake of being too

patronising and peremptory in their bargaining. When a bazaar storekeeper in the old city of Jerusalem asks, say, 10,000 shekels for a fine shawl it is tactless to make an immediate precise counter offer such as 'I'll give you five thousand' or to say, 'You must be joking!' It is better to say, 'Ten thousand is too much.' The storekeeper will, sooner or later, say, 'How much do you want to pay?' And the buyer can then legitimately say, 'No more than five thousand.' Also, a lot of tourist Westerners are rude and approach a purchase with a manner which says, 'I know all about the way you crooks operate and you're not going to fool me.' Many traders prefer not to sell at all rather than deal with somebody who displays ignorance and rudeness.

BEDOUIN

The term bedouin was used as a synonym for 'Arab' in the early societies of the Arabian peninsula, with the difference that 'bedouin' had a corollary meaning of 'raider'. Bedouin comes from the word 'Badawiyin', meaning originally people who lived in the open country and deserts.

Individualism was always a fundamental trait of the bedouin and it was accentuated by the harsh and depressing climate of the desert. It drove him into living in isolation and created his keen liking for 'freedom'.

The great Arab writer Ibn Khaldun,[7] whose opinions Arabs themselves respect, centuries ago assessed the bedouin, 'They are a savage nation, fully accustomed to savagery and the things that cause it. Savagery has become their character and their nature. They enjoy it, because it means freedom from authority . . . Furthermore the Bedouin are not concerned with laws or with deterring people from misdeeds or protecting people against others. They care only for . . . looting . . . It is noteworthy how civilisation always collapsed in places the Bedouin took and conquered.'

In modern times the nomadic bedouin are the free men of the Arab world and they are difficult subjects to rule. Because of their mobility and frequent raiding and skirmishing, the central government of each country long ago decided that it is better to let the nomads go their own way with a minimum of government interference. However, in each tribe the leader or sheikh exercises strict discipline; his right to rule is based partly on hereditary descent and partly on individual merit. Bedouin people have always idealised the proud man with a high sense of honour, hence the liking of certain tribes for T.E. Lawrence (Lawrence of Arabia).

In the desert no man can live alone; the bedouin is required by his harsh environmment to be a social animal. Resources are too scattered for large numbers of people to live together but efficient use of those resources requires team effort. Bedouin society has always been what William Polk[8] calls 'a pulsating organism', subject to rapid coagulation and to equally rapid disintegration. As one clan grows rich numerous other clans will ally themselves to it and it will absorb them. When it outruns its resources or becomes politically unwieldy the clan subdivides. There never have been large numbers of bedouin and today their numbers are decreasing. Reliable statistics do not exist but all the Arab countries together are unlikely to have more than a million bedouin.

Bedouin hospitality and protection for the traveller is proverbial and easily explained: Every bedouin knows that the time might come when he will need to seek shelter, food and protection from somebody else in the harshness of the desert, so he extends all this to strangers. Westerners are unlikely to meet bedouin though they could see their large goatskin tents at a distance from the road. They dislike contact with tourists and especially they do not want to be photographed. To photograph the women is considered especially offensive.

See HOSPITALITY

BEGIN, Menachem

Begin was born in Poland in 1913 and educated at Warsaw University; he was active in the Jewish Youth Movement, 'Betar', and was chairman of the organisation in Czechoslovakia in 1936 and in Poland in 1939. The Russian

NKVD (the secret police) imprisoned him in a Siberian labour camp in 1940 – 41 and when he was released he accompanied the Polish Free Army to Palestine in 1942. He became chief of Irgun Zvai Leumi in 1943 and was one of the leaders of the revolt against the British, who ruled Palestine under a United Nations mandate. He was a member of the 1st, 2nd, 3rd, 4th and 5th Knessets (Israeli parliament) and was minister without portfolio in the period 1967–70.

After he founded the Herut (Freedom) Party he grew more influential and in 1977 he became Prime Minister. The same year he signed a peace treaty with Egypt's president, Anwar Sadat, one of the most remarkable events in modern Middle East history. A courteous and courtly man of high principles, Begin suffered in world opinion because of his past as a 'terrorist'. He made Israel even stronger than it had been before and he was largely responsible for the 1982 invasion of Lebanon to drive the PLO from the southern part of the country. The massacres which took place in two Beirut refugee camps, when Phalangist Christian soldiers murdered hundreds of unarmed Palestinians, shocked him and he was even more disturbed when an Israeli commission of inquiry found that some senior Israeli officers were guilty of negligence. Despite unrest in Israel, Begin remained popular. The death of his wife in 1982 sapped much of his will, the war against the PLO and Syria undermined his health and he resigned in 1983. He will be remembered as the first Israeli Prime Minister who was able to induce an Arab leader to make peace.

BODY LANGUAGE

For Arabs at all social levels, gestures are an indispensable part of any conversation. To tie an Arab's hands while he is speaking is tantamount to tying his tongue. Robert Barakat, an anthropologist at Newfoundland Memorial University, gathered a dictionary of body language from throughout the Arab world and was able to give specific definitions to 247 movements and actions. The majority of gestures were obscene but many convey respectable and useful information. For instance, a man in Saudi Arabia will kiss the top of another man's head to signify apology. In Jordan and other countries to flick the right thumbnail against the front teeth means that the gesturer has little or no money. Bedouin touch their noses three times to show friendship.

In Libya it is customary for men to twist the tips of their forefingers into their cheeks when speaking to beautiful women, although this makes their faces appear contorted. Many gestures are tacit tools of flirtation. Northern Syrians blow smoke into a woman's face to show that they desire her but it is difficult to assess what effect this has on the lady. In Lebanon the same message is conveyed by punching the left palm with a closed right fist. All Arabs share a basic vocabulary of body language, according to Robert Barakat, and from my own observations he is correct. They stand close together and frequently touch one another during conversation, and they look each other in the eye constantly, instead of letting their gaze drift to the side as Westerners do. Nearly all gesturing is done with the right hand rather than the 'unclean' left.

While Arabs employ some Western gestures – they tease one another by sticking out their tongues – a few crucial gestures mean diametrically opposite things in the two cultures. When Arabs shake their heads from side to side they are saying yes instead of no. Moreover, when Arabs mean no they move the head upward – and click the tongue – and they would seem, in Western eyes, to be nodding assent. Barakat relates the story of an English teacher in a Middle East school whose wife had remained behind in England. When one of his Arab students left for a trip to England the teacher suggested that the young man call on his wife while there. The student did, and had an affair with the lonely woman. On returning home for a visit the Englishman asked his wife if the Arab had paid a call. Reacting guiltily, the wife denied having met the student – by snapping her head upward and clicking her tongue.

A Westerner can easily give unintentional offence, for instance by crossing his legs when in company and revealing the sole of his shoe; this is offensive because the movement implies that the person to whom the shoe points is beneath contempt. Offering a gift in the left hand might also be miscronstrued since it is an unclean hand to strict Muslims. It is also important to know when to laugh; it is wiser to allow the Arab to give a lead. When parting from an Arab it is always better to back away or move sideways, rather than turn your back since this too may be taken to mean that you are glad to be leaving him.

BRIBERY

Money changes hands as a matter of course in almost all dealing and in most negotiations with government and local government officials throughout the Middle East, except in Israel. In the West the very word bribery has connotations of dishonesty and corruption which would not be understood in the Middle East. While bribery is abnormal in the Western world – and can be heavily punished in the courts – in Arab countries it is the norm. It might be difficult for Europeans, schooled in ethics and morality, to accept this but until they do so they will not make progress in the Middle East business and commercial world.

Not only foreigners need to bribe their way through the bureaucratic network; local people also pay if they wish to receive 'favoured' treatment. It is easier to get a telephone, for instance, if the householder can pass money to the clerk who allots the phone. Queues for airline tickets can be jumped by the discreet passing of paper money to the desk clerk. Bribery in most Arab countries defies reform and money must be paid for each signature on a departmental form, the amount varying according to the bureaucratic importance of the official. Bribery is generally direct but sometimes it can operate in other ways. Should somebody offer to mind your parked car it is advisable to come to terms with him or on your return the tyres will at best be let down or more likely slashed.

Bribery among the nationals of a country is often conducted openly but the foreigner needs to adopt some technique. Money is best put in an envelope and handed to an official with the casual comment 'This may be relevant' or 'This is an important document.' If the amount is inadequate the official may return the envelope saying, 'This does not affect the matter.' Directors of ministries and even government ministers are entirely open to bribes but they like them to be offered at high level, from the vice-president of a company for instance. No direct conversation about bribes takes place and there is no mention of raw figures. The vice-president will say, 'Shall we say 5 per cent?' (that is, of the whole deal). And the minister will respond, 'Indeed, let us say that.' That's all there is to it. Many Western companies with offices in the Arab world employ a permanent native negotiator; he handles all the bribery so that the foreigners need not be involved. Not surprisingly, the negotiator himself exacts a bribe from the people with whom he is doing business.

Bribery is necessary for a good table in a restaurant and it eases problems with the police and with customs officials. I know many well-to-do Arabs and some foreigners who never wait in a customs or immigration queue; they walk straight to the head of the queue and say, 'Do you want to see my passport?' which they proffer with a finger holding down a wad of notes. In addition to bribery there is the ageless *baksheesh* (from which we get the English idiomatic word buckshee, meaning free). Baksheesh is demanded by boys and beggars in Middle East Muslim countries. To protect the tourist from harassment some governments have made it illegal but the practice is deeply rooted. When a tourist gives baksheesh to one boy scores more of them will follow him noisily and relentlessly through a bazaar.

Sometimes a scandal erupts when a great trading company is found to have bribed officials of an Arab country to agree to a deal. The outrage is unrealistic and does not take into account a completely different set of morals. Even physicians and surgeons can be bribed, not necessarily to provide better attention but certainly preferential treatment. I know an Egyptian doctor who keeps his poor patients waiting for hours in the waiting-room while he deals with those from whom he knows he can expect a 'favour'.

While most bribery takes the form of cash, a deposit placed in a foreign bank is equally acceptable. In the upper levels of society it is possible to bribe some men with gifts, such as an expensive car or diamonds or the favours of a desirable girl. Cautious Middle East officials prefer money to be passed outside the country and it is not uncommon for bribery to be in the form of 'a good time' in London, Paris, Brussels or Amsterdam. Those who come from countries where the rules of Islam are strictly enforced enjoy this form of bribery since it consists of gambling, alcohol, drugs, hot night clubs and women.

BRITAIN IN THE MIDDLE EAST

By the end of World War II in 1945 British influence, military, political and economic, was profound in Libya, Egypt, Palestine and Transjordan, Saudi Arabia, Aden and all the sheikhdoms of the Arabian (Persian) Gulf. This influence began to decline as Arab nationalism increased. The process quickened with the end of the mandate for Palestine – simultaneously with the foundation of Israel. After the 1956 Suez Crisis, which discredited Britain, it was clear that Britain's imperial days, at least in the Middle East, were ending. By withdrawing from Aden in November 1967 Britain signalled that it had begun the process of leaving the Persian Gulf. The process was complete by 1971, when Britain terminated treaties with the Trucial States (so called because of the truces which the British forced them to sign in the 19th century). No significant political vacuum was left as a result of the British departure since all the countries concerned became independent, with their own governments.

The 1960s and 1970s were bonanza decades in the Gulf and British capital was using its privileged position to grab as much of the new oil revenues as it could. In 1971 Britain still provided about 40 per cent of Oman's imports, 38 per cent of Qatar's, 31 per cent of Abu Dhabi's, 35 per cent of Dubai's and 12 per cent of Kuwait's. Also, despite the relative decline the absolute figures were rising. Massively effective but dubious trading operations were carried out by the semi-official Crown Agents. This institution, dating from 1833, was a purchaser for 250 foreign buyers including

70 governments. For its customers it spent in Britain up to £100 million a year and had up to £1,000 million of foreign cash in London for use in property and stock market speculation. It annually placed orders with about 15,000 British firms. One of its eight overseas offices was in Bahrain and all the Gulf governments used it. The Crown Agents were an important link in funnelling back oil revenues to Britain from the Gulf.

The Middle East countries have had a love-hate relationship with Britain. The Arabs largely blame Britain for the existence of the State of Israel although the British had gone to extreme lengths to stop what they termed 'illegal immigration' of Jews into Palestine. British companies, particularly those involved in oil development, have been accused of exploiting the Arab countries.

For many years Jordan was dependent on British subsidies but anti-British riots took place. While Libya was ruled by King Idris it was pro-British but the arrival of Colonel Gaddafi as president-dictator made the country the most anti-British in the Middle East. Syria, Iraq, the Yemen Arab Republic, Saudi Arabia and Egypt have at times been bitterly critical of British foreign policy.

On the whole Britain has enjoyed good relations with Middle Eastern countries and British business interests are widespread. Arabs treat British visitors with some reserve but are not usually hostile. Because of their political volatility and Islamic sensitivity the Arab states' attitudes can change overnight. An example was that of Saudi Arabia which objected to the British television programme *Death of a Princess*. The film depicted the stoning to death of a Saudi princess for adultery, and this execution had in fact happened. As a result Saudi-British relations were strained almost to breaking point. The election of Mrs Thatcher as Prime Minister in 1979 mystified the Arabs since it would not be remotely possible for a woman to reach such a position in the Arab world, but they came to respect her because they consider her to be a strong personality. Similarly the Queen has been accorded great public respect on her visits to Arab countries, other than in Morocco. Possession of a British passport no longer ensures that the holder will be given privileged treatment but a certain grudging respect is still offered.

BUSINESS

Doing business in the Arab Middle East is slow, formal and often tedious. Society is so conservative that reform is slow; indeed bureaucracy defies reform. Egypt is regarded as a progressive country but bureaucracy manages to drag down good intentions and to dull initiative by poor organisation and the sheer dead weight of paper work. Imported items often require accompanying forms two inches thick. For example, a foreign businessman who tried to get a piece of computer equipment out of customs at Cairo airport. 'We needed 56 signatures,' he said. 'I couldn't believe it until I saw the paper with 56 names on it. And we had to make payoffs right, left and centre to get them. But it's not over then. Once you have the names and you're on your way out the door any minor official can crook his finger and ask to examine the paper. If he's not satisfied with one of the signatures he sends you back and you have to start all over.'

It is essential for foreign companies to employ a local negotiator and a specialist in Arab and Islamic law.

While the EEC nations have done well in selling goods to the Middle East countries the Japanese have performed even better. They are prepared to meet any and every demand even if they have never before heard of a particular piece of equipment. Offering a competitive price and promising delivery, they then return to Japan to design and make the required goods, which are invariably delivered by the contract date. The Japanese also have the patience needed to do business in the Middle East without showing irritation or exasperation.

There are no difficulties with payments for exports to most Middle East countries. The exceptions are Syria, which has a perennial trade deficit, Sudan, where exports earnings cover less than half the imports bill, and Libya, where payment is often delayed because of complex bureaucracy. Iran, whose economic affairs are in ruins because of the war with Iraq, is living off its gold reserves. Iraq can pay its bills because of generous Saudi aid.

Arab businessmen and government officials prefer to do business with foreigners who are *obviously* wealthy. The director or agent who visits a capital city and stays at a three-star hotel is starting with a disadvantage compared with the man who chooses the Hilton, Sheraton or Intercontinental or any other superior hotel.

The foreign company with lords, knights and generals on the board also has an advantage, while such apparently little things as gold-embossed files and fine notepaper are noticed. Presentation matters quite as much as the product, though this does not mean that Middle East buyers are gullible. They paid vast sums for inferior goods in the 1960s and early 1970s but experience has made them much more cautious.

The most profitable trade is still in weapons systems, munitions and military equipment because the clever salesman plays on the Arabs' natural feeling of insecurity and on their pleasure in owning the latest and best in weapons. One well-known arms company made profits of thousands of millions of dollars by using the simple technique of don't-tell-your-neighbour. Their salesmen's line was: 'We are prepared to sell you the very latest in anti-aircraft defence and, provided you don't make this public, we will sell to you alone and not to other Middle East countries.' In fact, they sold the identical product to several states simply by changing the name of the system and altering the description of the product. A West German company sold river gunboats to Libya though the country has no rivers; an enterprising Frenchman sold Iraq a submarine which it does not need and for which it has no crew. At least in these cases the products were genuine; in others, arms swindles have been even more scandalous.

CHILDREN

Most Arabs raise their children according to fixed practice established over the centuries. Their ideal is to bring up children in exactly the same way that they themselves were brought up. Some educated urban Arabs are moving away from this pattern but the vast majority could not imagine themselves questioning the rightness of traditional ways. They would consider it strange, even bizarre, to go to doctors or books to learn how to bring up children.

A baby is like an object, tossed from one lap to another and fed by any wet nurse who happens to be there when he cries for his mother, who may not be available. Sania Hamady[4] says, 'As he grows the Arab child is not treated as an independent human being with autonomous desires and aversions. His talk is not listened to and his questions are silenced with "You are too young to understand". He is forced to be co-operative and left with no freedom to choose . . . Thus the child learns to do what he is told, to obey in order to avoid punishment and to hope for some positive reward.'

But there is no correlation of act and reward because of a double standard of roles – public and private – according to which a child's behaviour oscillates. He has to learn the nuances which various situations demand. The child can rely on no set behavioural pattern; he has to watch for any hint or gesture from his father or mother or any other member of the family.

Mistrust quite early becomes part of an Arab child's thought processes. A leading scholar of Arab life, G.E. Grunebaum,[10] says, 'It has been observed that each of the children who comes to [an Arab] school believes that no person, not even his father or mother, can be implicitly trusted; that every statement he hears has to be weighed. Never the simple reaction, "That's true," or "It isn't true." Never the simple remark, "That's interesting." Always, *Why did he say it? Why did he want me to hear it?'*

Male children are infinitely more highly prized than girls – yet many families dress their sons as girls until the age of five to keep evil eyes from focussing on them. Boys are the custodians of the family's name and honour; there is no continuity without them. Girls are a liability and a constant worry – in case they should lose their 'honour'; that is, they may cease to be virgins.

In most Arab societies a boy is superior to his mother, simply because he is male. He is pampered by his mother, his sisters, all female relations, and all female servants and he is permitted to dominate all the women of the household. Many Western observers have noticed how the servants will fondle a small boy's genitals, partly because they believe that he enjoys this handling.

In upper class and middle class homes a boy has great authority over the servants, some of whom endure much bullying. On one occasion I was a guest in a house where the youngest son, aged five, was mildly slapped by his father for consistently interrupting the adults while they were speaking. The little boy wandered sullenly around the house until he found a servant at the top of the stairs – so he pushed him violently down. The family was vastly amused; the father called his son a ruffian – but ruffled his hair affectionately. The servant, despite his rough, bruising fall, showed no resentment; he was probably used to such treatment.

The Westerner visiting an Arab home may take some small present for a small child and for a boy at any age; it is unwise for a man to give a girl a present once she has reached puberty since much more may be read into the gift than the visitor intended. Also, if he had been previously in the home, the girl could be accused of having 'made eyes' at the visitor; why else would he now give her a present?

When parents are divorced, and for men divorce is easily achieved, boys at the age of seven and girls at nine may be lawfully taken from the mother and brought to the father's house.

See FAMILY: SOCIETY

CHRISTIANS

A minority in the Middle East, Christians are a *dhimmi* or second-class people often subjected to harassment by

militant Muslims. They have fewer rights than Muslims and
some mullahs say that they have *no* rights, only the privilege
of being allowed to live in an Islamic country.

In a preface to an academic study on the role of
Christians,[9] Bishop Francis Sayre of Washington Cathedral
wrote:

> A black man in the United States knows what it is
> like to live as a minority. Perhaps he alone . . . can
> imagine what it is like to belong to a religious
> minority in a state that makes little distinction
> between God and government . . . A minority is
> often wounded . . . it requires special faith and skill
> . . . to persevere. Such has been the fate of Christians
> in the Muslim lands of the Middle East.

Christians have a built-in disadvantage: they follow a creed
which is based on humility and forgiveness which are poor
weapons against the more aggressive aspects of Islam. Since
Islam did not make its appearance until the 7th century AD it
follows that Christians (and Jews) were in the Middle East
long before Muslims but this does not gain them any
respect. Muhammad brought the 'final revealed word of
God' which superseded all previous religions; Christians
and Jews, Muslims say, have been remiss in not converting
to Islam.

Many more Christians live in the Middle East than Islam
likes to admit and in nearly all regions they are often among
the best educated and most cultured. It is virtually impossible for a Christian to have political authority and rare
enough for one to hold administrative authority but through
efficiency as bankers, lawyers and businessmen they do
have influence.

All of the Christian communions of the Arab lands, other
than Roman Catholics, permit marriage of the clergy, and
require celibacy only of their bishops and patriarchs, who
are usually drawn from monastics. The status of women in
the Christian communities is markedly higher than that of
Muslim women.

The Christian pattern of the Middle East is infinitely
complex in ecclesiastical, economic and political terms. A

general knowledge of Christian involvement in Middle Eastern affairs is vital to all visitors. Businessmen and journalists in particular should make a point of finding out the religion of the people with whom they are dealing. This helps greatly to discern and understand intention and attitude, prejudice and bias. For example, Greek Orthodox Christians tend to be pro-PLO while Greek Catholics are against that organisation. Again, in Syria and Lebanon the Orthodox families are on closer terms with the ruling Muslim establishment than most other Christians.

Scores of Christian creeds exist in the Middle East. Most significant are: Greek Orthodox, Greek Catholic, Syrian Orthodox (Jacobites), Syrian Catholic, Maronite, Copt, Coptic Catholic, Nestorian, Chaldean Catholic, Armenians, Latin and Protestant.

COPTS   The largest of the Christian groups, comprising what is officially called the Coptic Orthodox Church, Copts are found almost exclusively in the Nile Valley, where they number about 8 million, though some estimates say 10 million. Copts have long regarded themselves as the 'true Egyptians', the direct descendants of the Pharaonic race, but neither the State nor their Muslim compatriots give them this status.

Because the Egyptian government wants to maintain the image of Egypt as the leader of the Muslim Arab states, it has always admitted to fewer non-Muslims in the population than it really has. Also, many Copts in rural or heavily Muslim areas are reluctant publicly to confess Christianity when asked their religion by official census takers. Robert Brenton Betts, the greatest authority on Christians in the Middle East, pointed out that the obituary columns of Cairo's main daily paper carried more Coptic names than Muslim names, one indication of the large number of Copts.

COPTIC CATHOLIC   Though tracing its origins back to Saint Francis of Assisi's famous confrontation with the Ayyubid Sultan Al-Kamil in 1219, the Coptic Catholic Church has been officially in existence only since 1895 and has 100,000 members, mostly in Cairo.

NESTORIANS More often referred to today as Assyrians, the Nestorians are a remnant of what was once a great Christian body. By the 19th century barely 100,000 remained, mostly in the Zagros mountains of Iraqi Kurdistan. During World War I they fled *en masse* to the British lines for safety but 50,000 were massacred by the Turks and Kurds. Today 35,000 live in Iraq and north-eastern Iran and 15,000 in Syria and Lebanon.

CHALDEAN CATHOLIC An effective force only since 1834, the Chaldeans have grown from 20,000 to 200,000, most of them in Iraq where they are the largest Christian community. Because they avoid the deadly game of Iraqi politics they are reasonably secure. Another 11,000 live under oppression in Iran, 7,000 in Syria and 2,500 in Lebanon.

ARMENIANS Having adopted Christianity shortly before the Council of Nicaea in the early 4th century, the Armenians consider themselves to be the oldest Christian nation. Brutally treated in Turkey after World War I, the Armenians became refugees to the Arab countries and 200,000 now live in Lebanon, their numbers swollen by emigration from Syria and Egypt where their religion makes them unwelcome. Though still barely Arabicised, the Armenian community as a whole is becoming in each succeeding generation more and more a part of its Arab environment.

LATIN AND PROTESTANT On the fringe of Arab Christendom are the small communities of native followers of the Catholic and Protestant rites of the West. Almost entirely urban, well-educated and strongly Western oriented, the Arab Latin Rite Catholics number about 110,000, with major centres in Jerusalem, Bethlehem, Beirut, Cairo, Aleppo, Haifa and Nazareth. Possibly three times the Latins in number, the Arab Protestants with their tradition of liberal education represent 'the most progressive and Westernised element', according to the American scholar, Raphael Patai.[23] In Lebanon and Syria the Protestants are predominantly Presbyterian, in Israel and Jordan they are Anglican; of the roughly 300,000 native Protestants in Egypt close to 200,000 are of Coptic ancestry.

MARONITES The Maronites are unique among Christian communities in the Middle East because they alone are confined to one major geographical concentration – Lebanon – and they alone possess absolute religious and political unity. They have long recognised the authority of the Roman pope but in many ways they are ecclesiastically independent. Politically, they are solidly Lebanese nationalist and markedly pro-French in culture. Prosperous, educated and dedicated to their community, the Maronites are very much what a famous Lebanese statesman, Charles Malik, called them, 'the Christian answer to Islam.' Many have left Lebanon because of the conflicts which have ravaged that country since 1975 but probably 700,000 remain.

SYRIAN CATHOLIC   About 90,000 Syrian Catholics live in Lebanon, Egypt, Iraq and in Syria itself. Under their own patriarch, they are educated, prosperous and vital people. They are not subject to the authority of Rome.

SYRIAN ORTHODOX (Jacobite) The Syrian Orthodox community of Lebanon, Syria and Iraq numbers about 175,000, a small but important remnant of the once powerful Monophysite church of Syria. Formerly a rural community, they have become urbanised since the 1920s and their patriarch lives in Beirut – when that city is at peace.

GREEK CATHOLIC   Next to the Maronites, the Greek Catholics (or Melkites) are the largest and most prosperous Christian community in the Middle East, with 250,000 in Lebanon, Jordan, Syria and Israel; another 7,500 live in Egypt. They are particularly noted for the high standard of education among laity and clergy. Their patriarch has his seat in Damascus.

GREEK ORTHODOX   Historically divided among the ancient patriarchates of Antioch, Jerusalem and Alexandria, the modern Orthodox population is today concentrated in the first two. The patriarch of Alexandria is a Greek who ministers to a predominantly Greek community of less than 50,000 in Egypt. The patriarch of Jerusalem, also a Greek, presides over 85,000 native Arab-speaking Greek Orthodox worshippers of Israel and Jordan. A good many of these people are Palestinians living on the West Bank and they are singularly well educated. The patriarch of Antioch, an Arab and traditionally resident in Damascus, heads a prosperous community of Syrian and Lebanese Orthodox Christians. The patriarchate has long been a political battleground between a leftist faction backed by the Soviet Union through the Russian Orthodox Church and a succession of left-wing Syrian governments, and a strong pro-West element in Lebanon and abroad. The principal Orthodox centres are Beirut, Damascus, Tripoli and Lebanon.

Christianity in the Arab countries still believes in miracles, apparitions and visitations. One of the most recently documented miracles occurred in the summer of 1970 when 'the Virgin hovered over the Jacobite church in the Musaytba quarter of Beirut for three consecutive nights.' Thousands of Lebanese claim to have witnessed the event. A miraculous tale was widely circulated in Beirut in September 1975 at the outbreak of Christian-Muslim hostilities and it was given great credence. A Maronite taxi-driver picked up a heavily cloaked woman one evening during a lull in the fighting. She sat in the rear and asked to be taken to a point in the centre of the shooting and when the driver demurred she offered a 100-pound note (about £35). During the trip the driver spoke worriedly about the trouble in Lebanon. The lady quietly assured him that by Christmas 'the forces of Christ' would triumph and 'everything will be as it was before.' When the driver looked around the lady had vanished – and he swore that he had not slowed down and that he had not heard the door open or close. Word of this apparition quickly spread – but Christmas 1975 came and went with some of the heaviest fighting to that time.

CIVIL WARS

Middle East history is largely made up of civil or internal wars. Since 1945 virtually every Middle Eastern country has endured at least one such war; even Israel came close to one in 1948 when David Ben Gurion, as the first prime minister, had to demonstrate his authority over the ultra nationalists led by Menachem Begin.

Often a civil war has been the result of plots hatched by outsiders, as in the case of Jordan in 1970 and Lebanon 1975–85. In both instances the PLO was a major irritant. In other cases religion has been the cause, as with Iran in 1979–80. In yet other instances the forces of nationalism have driven certain groups to war against the state. The Kurds of Iran and Iraq have waged intermittent civil war against their respective regimes for decades. Sudanese Muslims and Christians have been in conflict. Iraq, Syria, Algeria, Cyprus, both the Yemens and some of the Gulf states have suffered civil war while Saudi Arabia, Libya, Tunisia, and Morocco have narrowly averted it. Civil war seems to be inevitable – and could almost be regarded as 'normal' – in countries which have dictatorships, absolute monarchies and oligarchies – and this applies to a large proportion of the Arab world, Iran and Turkey.

See DICTATORSHIP: GOVERNMENT

CLIMATE

It is too easy to generalise about Middle East climate as hot, dry and sunny. This describes much of the area between April and the end of October, though March and October are generally temperate. A significant climatic factor is the great difference between day and night temperatures in countries which have little cloud cover to keep in the daytime heat. In the desert, nights can be bitterly cold even in summer and many visitors have found that they cannot spend an entire holiday in very light clothing. Altitude too has a marked effect; Jerusalem, at a height of 2,000 feet, can be cool even on an August evening. The summer can be taken more or less for granted but the region does indeed have a winter, especially away from the coast. The mountains of Israel and Lebanon can be cool and misty and those of Iraq, Turkey and Iran are often snow-covered.

Throughout the Middle East rain falls during the winter though it is rarely heavy. Contrasts can be extreme and interesting when countries have mountains close to the coast, as Lebanon has. It is possible to swim and to ski (or at least to be amid snow) on the same morning in spring. People from temperate and maritime climates visiting the Middle East during the summer often attempt to do more than is comfortably possible in the great and enervating heat. Because of humidity, coastal cities such as Tel Aviv and Tripoli are particularly trying. By noon everywhere it is sensible to be indoors and there is no appreciable cooling before 4 p.m. During summer virtually all government offices start work at 7 a.m. and close by 2 p.m.

COMMUNITY

In Middle Eastern culture the uniformity of the citizens of a country as a whole is not emphasised; uniformity within each special segment or community is much more important. Many Western politicians do not understand the importance of community ties among Middle East people but lump them together as, say, Egyptians and Libyans or even more generally as Arabs.

The Middle East has a great diversity of ethnic units and each one feels the need to identify itself by some set of symbols. If by virtue of their history they possess some special racial characteristic they will enhance it by say, special haircuts – as do the orthodox Jews of Mea Sherim in Jerusalem. A group will wear distinctive garments, as do the Druze, or behave in a distinctive fashion, as upper class Saudis do. Anybody conversant with the sets of symbols has no difficulty when walking through a bazaar in identifying members of the various communities; Middle Eastern people want to be identified and they make identification easy.

Arabs are easily irritated when referred to as 'Arabs'; a man will tell a foreigner that he is an Alawite Syrian or a

Christian Jordanian, a Copt from Egypt, a Maronite Lebanese or an Iranian Kurd. Even if he uses a simplistic label such as Libyan, Algerian or Saudi when speaking with foreigners, he will use the name of his tribe or family when with other Arabs. The sense of community is so strong that for most people of the Arab world their first loyalty is to that community. Lebanon is a classic example. The country is peopled by Sunni Muslims, Shi'a Muslims, Druze, Maronite Christians, Greek Orthodox Christians and several other groups, and without exception their respective members give their first allegiance to their community. After that they are members of the Lebanese nation, apart from the Maronites, who deny that they are Arabs; they are not even Lebanese Arabs, just Lebanese. Even more, they say, they are the *first* Lebanese since they are descended from the Phoenicians who once inhabited this land. Similarly, many Egyptians do not consider themselves to be Arabs. 'I am an Egyptian, neither more nor less,' a university professor once told me irritably. 'Do not class me with the Arabs.'

In Israel there are signs of a dual community – that of the Ashkenazi or Jews of European extraction and the Orientals, those Jews who lived in Arab lands as nationals of those countries before they were driven out as refugees. Cyprus has the same phenomenon with Turkish Cypriots and Greek Cypriots; the sense of community of both groups is so aggressive that they are hostile to each other and each claims precedence over the other.

Society throughout the Middle East is a conglomeration of thousands of communities with only a functional trust between any two. Within the borders of any one country the various communities co-operate because they have more to gain that way, but there is only a limited sense of belonging to a nation. In Arab armies each unit is, as far as possible, formed from men from the same tribe for the sake of morale and to reduce the risk of tensions which would result if men came from mixed tribes.

COPTS

See CHRISTIANS

CORRUPTION

Corruption is so commonplace in Middle East society that it is the norm; it is therefore difficult and perhaps unfair to make comparisons with Europe and the West generally. Bribes, favours, inducements, 'percentages', nepotism, inflated estimates – the whole arsenal of corruption is simply normal business and should not be too readily condemned. A basic reason for this attitude is that lower and middle order clerks and officials, in government and private service, have always been lowly paid. Traditionally they were forced to cheat in various ways just to get enough money to support themselves and their families. Indirectly, greedy imperialist merchants encouraged their workers to indulge in corruption. Also, the foreign merchants themselves were often corrupt and this example infected the nationals who worked for them.

In modern times the State provides little protection for its citizens in poverty, sickness or old age so again they get their money where and how they can and hoard it against the day of crisis. Monarchs, presidents, prime ministers, ministers of state and leading businessmen – most are corrupt by European standards. The insecurity inherent in Arab life has led men to think of money as their refuge. It is no secret in the upper levels of society that leaders hide millions of dollars in banks abroad. Nor is it a secret that many of the great multinational companies which operate in the Middle East budget large amounts to be spent in the network of corruption. Before the foreign oil companies were nationalised they spent about 10 per cent of their profits on payments to high officials as 'consultancy fees'. Consultancy often took the form of protecting the companies against the threat of nationalisation and governmental demand for a higher percentage of the profits.

Libya seethed with corruption from the time that oil was found in vast quantity in the mid-1950s. The inexperienced king, Idris, was no match for the foreign oil company agents who flocked to his palace with concession contracts. He delegated the responsibility for granting concessions to government ministers whose venality and corruption were unbridled. For ten years the country gushed oil under financial terms that were patently unfair to the country as a whole though highly profitable to individual ministers.

Instead of granting widespread exclusive concessions the ministers realised that more personal, under-the-table income would be derived by playing the old established companies off against the newer, smaller independent operators who were entering the Middle East oil venture. Thus, they parcelled out several districts among the major companies and the independents for large advances but at royalty and tax schedules that were well below the norm of the Gulf countries.

By paying further bribes, the oil companies persuaded the Libyan ministers to keep their country out of OPEC for as long as possible so as to maintain their low oil payments. Pressures from the other states became too great, Libya joined OPEC and the companies were forced to pay rates on a par with those in the Gulf. The new rates did not end Libyan corruption which was responsible for Libya's continued shipments of oil to Germany, where much of it was reshipped to Britain during the 1967 boycott. The Libyan oil boom after 1967 incited further corruption. With high government officials in the van, civil servants, police, customs agents and others in positions of petty authority all demanded higher and higher bribes. By 1969 'the Land of the Date Palm' – as Libya was calling itself for tourists – had become, to foreign oil men, 'the Land of the Greased Palm.'

From 1953 King Saud made Saudi Arabia a bizarre marvel of grotesque extravagance, with immense quickly built concrete palaces, glittering with gold and neon and housing his hundred successive wives. The confidence tricksters of the Arab world descended upon Riyadh and ensnared the royal family in an ever expanding web of corruption and fraud. Thousands of Saudi princes ventured to the West, spent fortunes on women, whisky and gambling, and returned with Cadillacs and highpriced European courtesans by the dozen. The monarchy was bankrupt by 1958 and the king brought in his half-brother, Faisal, as prime minister to put the country back on its feet.

Nepotism is a major part of Middle East corruption and it too is explicable in terms of survival. Any man assuming a position of power and authority feels safer if he recruits key personnel from among his relatives. For instance, President Assad of Syria has retained power because a relation has always controlled the secret police and the presidential bodyguard. Any official will do his best to appoint brothers, sons or cousins under him – nearly always for a fee. He hopes that his own position will be stronger and more permanent with the support of family members who owe him their jobs. The foreigner in the Middle East should always be careful about criticising one official to another; they are probably related. It is possible for one family to dominate an entire government or local government department.

In some Arab countries even airline employees are corrupt. For instance, a businessman arrives at Riyadh airport for a flight to Karachi on which he has booked a seat, and the clerk tells him, 'Unfortunately there was some accidental double-booking. It may have been a fault in the computer. We are very sorry. There is no seat for you.' If the businessman has Middle East experience he will hand over some money – perhaps the equivalent of 50 dollars. He might even say, 'Perhaps this will repair the computer fault.' Almost certainly a seat will magically become available. This exercise in petty corruption will not take place, usually, at a crowded check-in counter. Those clerks who use it are unlikely to exploit the ordinary tourist because they realise that a tourist does not know the rules of the game. He will fail to offer money and perhaps will become very angry. Many European and American businessmen, travelling on healthy expenses, invariably hand over their airline tickets with money simply to eliminate any possibility of 'no seat being available'.

Sania Hamady[4] says that 'among Arabs the feeling that any regulation may be circumvented [by bribery] is prevalent.'

See BUSINESS: BRIBERY

CRIME

Crime in the Middle East is viewed with more resignation than in the West because victims know from experience that the police do not catch most criminals. Three types of crime are distinguishable – against the State, against Islam and against society. In some countries, such as Saudi Arabia, those crimes against Islam are punished most severely, while in others, such as Syria, those against the State are most heinous. Crimes against society, such as burglary, assault, damage to property, are accepted as inevitable and punishment is severe – when a criminal is caught.

Crimes against Islam include the drinking of alcohol, indecorous dress (only women face this charge), adultery, failure to close business premises during hours of prayer. Of course, these offences might also be crimes against the laws of the state but the laws themselves are Koranic. Religious police enforce many of the regulations concerning public behaviour; for instance, in Saudi Arabia they carry long canes with which they will slash a woman exposing her ankles or arms. Shopkeepers might get a cane cut for being slow in closing their shutters at prayer times. But these are mild punishments compared with stoning to death or beheading for adultery; again, only women are so punished. A male adulterer may be whipped though not executed, since it is assumed that the woman led him astray, but rapists are sometimes executed. Rape is probably more frequently committed than is officially admitted because victims remain silent; to report the attack will expose the woman to shame for the rest of her life. Nobody supports a rape victim in Arab lands; she becomes an outcast.

Other crimes of violence are common, especially in urban areas. The criminals are usually the poor and the victims are wealthy. But violence in the course of bank robberies, so common in the West, is rare in Arab countries because all banks have armed guards – and they will shoot to kill.

The Arab regard for personal property is profound and punishment for theft can be harsh; even today Saudi Arabian justice demands that a thief has his right hand cut off. This is not always done but the lesser penalty of being kept in a Saudi gaol is bad enough. Despite the penalties theft is commonplace and visitors are particularly vulnerable, especially to pickpockets. Valuables should never be left in hotel bedrooms, even in what the visitor believes is a cleverly chosen safe hiding place, such as in a plastic bag in the toilet cistern.

Murder is so frequent in Arab countries that a violent death is worth only a few lines in the newspapers. Police chiefs have told me that most murders are never reported as such simply because there is no possibility of finding the murderer; often there is no chance of even identifying the victim because most ordinary people do not carry any identity and because few families report to the police when one of its members does not come home. When the police find a body it is easier for them to classify the case as 'death from natural causes' or as an 'accident', even when the victim has obviously been murdered.

CYPRUS

Because of hostility between Greek Cypriots and Turkish Cypriots the island has not known real peace in 20 years and *de facto* partition in 1974 merely brought increased tensions. In that year the 'Turkish Federated State of Cyprus' in the north divided itself from the Greek-Cypriot section. The

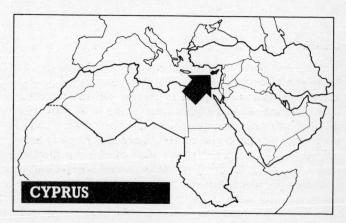

CYPRUS

Turks control about 36 per cent of the land area of 9,251 sq. km. and a fifth of the population of 660,000. At the time of partition 180,000 Greek Cypriots moved to the south and 45,000 Turkish Cypriots went to the north. An uneasy peace was preserved by the presence of a UN-patrolled buffer zone. In November 1983 the whole future of the island was put in the balance when the Turkish north, under its leader Rauf Denktash, declared itself completely independent.

Neither part of Cyprus is economically viable without the other and great imbalances exist. Inflation in the south was 6·5 per cent in 1984, in the north it was 20 per cent. The economy in the north is based on agriculture and tourism while in the south manufacturing and tourism have been developed more rapidly and are the mainstays of the economy. The economic embargo between north and south and the Turkish sector's lack of international recognition has yet to close economic links between the north and Turkey. Britain maintains two bases in Greek Cyprus, at Akrotiri and Dhekelia.

Arab states have a keen interest in Cyprus and the PLO has a major headquarters in Nicosia, Greek Cyprus, mostly for communications and propaganda. Except in times of crisis Cyprus is an agreeable place for Western tourists and it is easy enough for visitors to cross the 'Green Line' between north and south.

DEMOCRACY

Western democracy means government by the people in being able to elect by secret ballot, from a choice of people and parties, their own representatives for parliament, at the upper national level, and councils, at the local level. No dictatorships can develop because the president or prime minister or premier is also elected. Again, no one party may hold power for longer than specified by the constitution without again submitting to election. No one person – American president, British prime minister, French president – can rule without parliament (or its equivalent). All politicians are subject to criticism by the news media and the parliamentary opposition parties. No Arab government in the Middle East meets these requirements. (Lebanon was a democracy until 1975.) All states do have a parliament of sorts but in most cases there is only one party.

The elective principle was never genuinely followed in Islamic governments so the community could not acquire the experience normally associated with that principle – 'toleration of the unsuccessful by the successful,' as Harvard professor Morroe Berger[11] expresses it. Traditional governments did not practise such toleration and the rights and duties of majority and minority have never been clearly defined. Neither the majority nor the minority has permitted the other to perform its functions in a stable manner; the majority suppresses the minority, while the minority seeks by equally questionable means to depose the majority.

More than a century ago Western powers introduced 'legislative councils' into their Arab domains for no other purpose than to demonstrate to the Arabs how a modern state is run. They did not intend these councils as oppositions, but this is precisely what the Arabs made of them – a focus of native opposition to foreign rule. In thus challenging the authority of government the Arab leaders weakened the foreign regimes in the eyes of the ordinary people, who did not understand that it was possible to criticise government but still be obedient to it. Now the leaders of independent Arab states feel as the foreign rulers they ejected did – that official recognition of an Opposition would imply approval of what it might say or do.

Where the public does not understand the role of an Opposition it moves towards disobedience of the government. The public sees the Opposition as a competing power, not merely as a party competing *for* power. So governments suppress opposition to demonstrate that their authority may not be challenged with impunity. Against attitudes such as this the parliamentary system must fail.

The Arab economist Charles Issawi says that Arab countries also lack the basis for socio-economic democracy. The Arab states are at a disadvantage, he demonstrates, in the large size of their territory and population, their high birth rate, type of economy, distribution of wealth, low level of education, lack of patterns of co-operation and not least, in the restraints imposed by the Islamic religion.

In some countries a sense of democracy exists at village level in that an election takes place for the administrative council but it is not by secret ballot; this inevitably leads to many abuses, including coercion.

See DICTATORSHIP: GOVERNMENT

DEMOGRAPHY

Population statistics for the Middle East are neither complete nor wholly reliable. In some countries no full census has ever been taken and in many cases the most recent census was held several years ago. Even growth rates are uncertain because no complete register of births, deaths and migration exists. The figures given here are based on United Nations estimates.

The Middle East covers an area of 14·4 million square kilometres with a total population of about 260 million, which is perhaps 5 per cent of the world total. National populations range from less than 700,000 for the United Arab Emirates to more than 45 million in Turkey and in Egypt. With something like 20 people per sq. km. overall the region is one of moderate density. However, the inhabitants are very unevenly distributed between and within the political units which make up the area.

Zones of highest density with more than 100 people to the sq. km. are of two kinds – along major rivers and where there is enough water to support intensive rain-fed agriculture. Egypt is the prime example of the first kind; the settled zone of the country is almost wholly confined to the valley and delta of the Nile; densities are as high as 2,200 per sq. km. In central Iraq densities of several hundred per sq. km. are recorded in the valleys of the Tigris and Euphrates. The other type of high density population inhabits the Black Sea coast of Turkey, the Caspian coast of Iran, the Eastern Mediterranean or Levant coast (Syria, Lebanon, Israel) and parts of the lowlands of the Maghreb (Morocco, Algeria and Tunisia). In these areas densities are usually about 50 – 100 per sq. km. rising above 100 only in a few districts.

The majority of Middle Eastern countries have a long tradition of urban life but by Western European standards their level of urbanisation is still low. In some countries only a small minority live in towns: Yemen Arab Republic 7 per cent, Saudi Arabia 18 per cent, Sudan 13 per cent. Highest of all is Bahrain with 78 per cent. Despite the low general level the Middle East has 10 cities with more than a million inhabitants: Cairo at least 9 million, Teheran 4·5, Baghdad 3·3, Alexandria 2·8, Casablanca 2, Istanbul 2·7, Ankara 1·7, Algiers, Tunis and Damascus each more than 1 million.

A major feature of the region is the rapid rate of population growth. In practically every country death rates have fallen to less than 20 per 1,000 per year while birth rates are very high at more than 40 per 1,000, giving annual growth rates of between 2·5 and 4·5 per cent. As a result, populations are youthful, with 40 per cent under the age of 15. The growth in Egypt – at least 1 million more mouths to feed each year – is alarming; the country could not grow enough food for its people when the population was only 30 million.

International migration plays only a small part in population growth except in a few special cases. Qatar and Kuwait, for example, where the annual growth rate is 8 and 6 per cent respectively, reflect large-scale immigration. More than half the population of Kuwait are foreigners. Libya's population grew from less than 2 million in 1970 to 3 million in 1980 but this too reflects immigration. Israel's population reached 4 million in 1982, a density of more than 185 per sq. km.

DESERTS

Something needs to be said about deserts, not geographically but psychologically. Nearly all Middle East countries have large areas of desert, whether they are sand-seas, hard and stony ground, or barren, eroded mountains. Some countries, such as Egypt, exist despite deserts; others, such as Syria, have grown up around oases; yet others, such as Libya, are forced by deserts to cling to the coast. Israel, at great expense and effort, has made some of its deserts fertile.

A desert offers no security and living in a desert or on its fringes has been a major factor in making Arabs an insecure people. The genuine nomads have adapted to the desert and are part of it but other Arabs are aware of it as a kind of threat. Many foreigners resident in Arab countries have noted how their city Arab friends are distressed by and even frightened of the desert when in it for too long. I have travelled in the Libyan desert with city Libyans who underwent remarkable personality changes in the sand-sea. They became irritable and unstable, suspicious and inattentive and they asked repeatedly about directions – 'Are you sure this is the right direction?' – and about water. When we reached a city they returned to normal.

For many centuries to step outside the oasis or to move too far away from a river was courting disaster and though a lot of water can now be carried on a journey or simply provided by turning on a tap the racial insecurity of the dry desert has residual effects. For the foreign traveller the Middle East's deserts no longer pose the danger they once did; some tour operators run regular trips right across the Sahara from north to south. Water discipline still needs to be exercised but emergency supplies are available in many places. Many Europeans do not realise that the desert at night can be cold even in summer; without cloud cover the heat is quickly dissipated.

See CLIMATE

DESIRES

Middle Eastern people are creatures of the senses and therefore of their desires. However, the type of life ordained by the Koran and by the conservative traditions which permeate Arab and Persian societies prevent most people from gratifying their desires. For instance, alcohol is forbidden but many Arabs and Persians have a desire for strong drink. Since the sexes are strictly segregated normal male-female relationships cannot develop and sexual desires must be stifled. Thus they become more intense. Among younger people exists a profound and impatient desire for a 'better life' – the sort of life they see in foreign films. This desire is frustrated by unemployment and poverty. In Iran all desires, by decree of the ruling mullahs, are unhealthy, immoral and illegal. Middle Eastern peoples have the same desires as people anywhere; the great difference lies in the way their desires are expressed or stifled.

See KORAN: LOVE AND SEX

DICTATORSHIP

Arab countries have for many centuries been ruled by despots, even when those despots were foreign viceroys or governors. With independence, the rulers have been either king-dictators or military dictators or, in a few instances, civilian dictators thrown up by revolution. Since Arab peoples are highly individualistic it might seem strange, at first glance, that dictators can flourish. In fact, they prosper precisely because of the fierce individualism which permeates society. Morroe Berger[11] says, 'The passion for individual equality outside the political realm is not merely compatible with despotic government but may even require it.'

Strong individualistic and egalitarian tendencies, when not stabilised in voluntary associations playing accepted political roles, can constitute a perpetual challenge to government authority. Dictators must maintain their command by force or their power and authority will be eroded. This is very clear in the cases of military dictators Assad of Syria, Gaddafi of Libya and Nimieri of the Sudan and king dictator Hussein of Jordan. Few of the dictators of the Middle East have ever taken a step towards seeking compromise and consensus with competing personalities or groups in their respective countries. Should the dictator see a single man or a group as a threat he will banish, imprison or execute them. Since 1945 this has happened repeatedly throughout the Middle East. Even in Turkey, where General Evren became a reluctant dictator after the failure of democratic government, politicians who might cause trouble have been 'internally exiled' and forbidden to engage in politics on threat of harsher punishment. In more extreme countries – and perhaps Libya is the most extreme – opponents of dictatorship vanish. Israel, Lebanon and Cyprus have had no dictatorships, though Archbishop Makarios came close to being a dictator in Cyprus.

An Arab proverb states, 'Govern the rabble by opposing them.' The caliphs and sultans did just this in earlier times; their power was total and absolute. Modern rulers might call themselves by different titles, such as president, and they may go through the motions of delegating power, as Sadat, Mubarak, Gaddafi, Saddam Hussein and Bourguiba have done, but all decisions rest with them and they have often countermanded orders of their subordinates.
See DEMOCRACY: GOVERNMENT

DRESS

The Arab throws off his native garb and puts on Western clothes much more readily than, say, the Indians and Pakistanis. In clothes (as well as in speech and manners) the accultured Arab behaves in an ultra-westernised fashion and those with money buy their clothes in Western capitals. Even at political and economic meetings held in Arab capitals nearly all the men present, except the Saudis, wear Western dress. The Saudis retain traditional dress to emphasise their distinctiveness, though such Westernised personalities as Sheikh Yamani, the Saudi oil minister, wear these garments only in their own countries.

In Saudi Arabia and Iran and in parts of all Arab countries women must be veiled except in the presence of their husbands or close male relatives. Iranian society was liberal under the Shah and only older women in the more remote towns wore the shapeless *chador*, but the Khomeini regime brought back full covering for women. Their ankles and wrists and the lower part of the face must be covered and fingers should be concealed as much as possible.

While these restrictions seem extreme to Western minds it is nevertheless important for Western visitors to be decorous in dress. Arab men delight to see Western women in brief shorts and sun tops but they will certainly not respect them. Women so dressed, by Arab reasoning, must be immoral. In Israel women are given much more latitude in dress, except in the Orthodox communities, but no woman would enter a church in shorts or without her shoulders and arms being covered. Indeed, she would be refused entry.

Arab men are easily provoked and in some places women who dress to reveal and emphasise rather than to conceal make themselves vulnerable. Beirut, Tripoli, Khartoum and Cairo are difficult cities for a woman alone.

Despite the heat, men do not wear shorts in public except in Israel and Cyprus and even here they are the exception. Only on a beach or a kibbutz can a large number of men be found in shorts. Shorts on male visitors are tolerated in most countries but disliked in strictly Islamic ones and forbidden in Iran. Even in liberal Israel a man wearing shorts is refused admittance to the holy places. The garment is not considered respectful. Except on the beach Arab, Israeli, Turkish, Iranian and Cypriot men do not go topless; the sight of a man bare to the waist, so common in Western Europe, is considered repugnant and an offence to decency.

Arabs are somehow able to wear suits without apparent discomfort when both temperature and humidity are high. They are protected, perhaps, by their unshakeable conservatism. One of the most popular proverbs is 'Eat for yourself but dress for others.'

DRUZE SECT

The Druze people are members of a Muslim political and religious sect founded in 1040. Druze is from the Arab word *Duruz* and emanates from Ismail al-Durazi, founder of the sect; his name, al-Durazi, means 'the tailor'. The Druze live principally in the mountains of Lebanon, with smaller numbers in Israel and Syria.

The inner secrets of the Druze faith are kept from all but a few initiates. Alongside elements borrowed from Islam – such as belief in the one-ness of God and not in a trinity – the Druze confess to beliefs normally incompatible with Islamic theology, notably in the reincarnation of the spirit after death. Centuries ago the Druze were given permission by a leader to pretend outwardly to belong to the faith of the 'unbelievers' with whom they dwell. This safety measure for a minority people persists to the present, though it is less frequently exercised.

The Druze people are intelligent, self-respecting and generally hospitable; but they can be cruel – and by Western standards, treacherous. The women, though, have many rights not normally given to Arab women; for instance, they join the men at religious functions, they may initiate divorce proceedings and polygamy is forbidden.

About 200,000 Druze live in Lebanon, 100,000 in Syria and 50,000 in Israel. Only in Israel do they have complete freedom, including their own religious courts. In Lebanon the Druze have been in conflict with the Christians for centuries and in 1860 they massacred 12,000 Maronite Christians in a dispute over land.

EDUCATION

The great majority of people in the Middle East are illiterate and innumerate. Great efforts are being made to give most children at least a primary education, but the peasant and labouring classes have hardly yet been drawn into the educational process and most Arab children see little if anything of formal schools.

All schools, from those in villages with one teacher to the large modern institutions in cities, emphasize obedience and memorization. Traditionally, education meant being able to memorise the Koran and then recite it; the earlier a boy could do this the more prestige his family acquired from his 'education'. From this root came the peculiarly Islamic concept of education as being founded on memory. Students at all levels memorise entire chapters of textbooks and many can recite a given page – from the broken sentence at the beginning to the broken sentence at the end. But they are quite unable to answer questions on what they have read. In any case, pupils and students and their parents resent questions from the teacher. Their attitude is that the teacher's job is to tell, not to ask. The idea of learning through questioning has no relevance in many parts of the Middle East.

Arab governments have begun to build schools that encourage spontaneity and freedom in learning but this movement has not gone far, for freedom and recreation are looked upon as 'unbecoming'. Play is tolerated only outside the home and school and is expected to end with adolescence.

Even in countries where education of girls has never been considered necessary, as in Saudi Arabia, girls are now in school and a few reach university level. All direct teaching is done by women as a man is not permitted to teach girls – except through closed circuit television.

Under the Shah, Iran had an enlightened educational system but the revolution and the coming of Khomeinism destroyed it; in particular girls are taught merely the rudimentary skills expected of women in a strictly Islamic society. Teheran University had 23,500 students studying a choice of 108 courses under the Shah; in 1984 the number of students had shrunk to 4,000 and only six courses were available. All women lecturers have been sacked and girl students are limited to 400. Turkey gives its children a sound education though relatively few continue in school beyond the age of 14. In Israel, education is valued above all else and 40 per cent of people can now expect a university education, one of the highest proportions in the world.

In countries with an exceptionally high birth-rate, such as Egypt, there is no possibility of training enough teachers or building enough schools to cope with the burgeoning population. Libya, with a small population and the money to pay the salaries of imported teachers, is giving most of its people an education.

For many years the Arab states were handicapped by a shortage of trained administrative and technical personnel. Students showed little interest in the practical sciences but many qualified in law. Upon graduation, the legally trained men turned to the government for civil service posts, traditionally a preserve for the upper classes and from the 1960s for the middle class as well. Today the emphasis placed on science and technology has greatly increased as countries have embarked on industrialisation. In Egypt in 1961, 38,000 students had graduated over the previous decade in the natural sciences and technology from Egyptian faculties. In 1970 – 71, 86,412 students were enrolled in these fields and 22,000 were graduating annually. In 1980 – 81 more than 160,000 were enrolled and about 43,000 were graduating each year. These figures are not reflected in Sudan, Algeria, Syria, Iraq, Saudi Arabia or the Yemens.

See EGYPT: IRAN: ISRAEL: WOMEN

EGYPT

With a present population of 47 million increasing by 3 per cent annually Egypt will have 90 million people by the year 2000. More than 3,000 people live on each square mile of land on which life can be sustained – one of the highest population densities in the world. In fact, the entire population lives on 4 per cent of the land. These statistics are at the heart of all Egypt's problems. For instance, while the land of the Nile Delta is highly productive and can be cropped year-round, the exploding population constantly cuts exports and makes Egypt an importer of wheat and other basic foodstuffs.

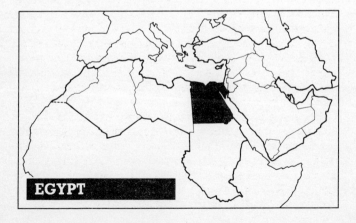

EGYPT

Above 85 per cent of the work force is employed by the government. In December 1982 President Mubarak told his parliament, 'We cannot overlook the present rate of population growth. It obstructs development efforts. It stands in the way of improving the living conditions of our people.' With a foreign debt of 13·5 billion dollars – which will rise to 16·5 billion by 1987 – the problems are daunting.

Other violent forces could do more damage to Egypt than the population explosion. President Mubarak is worried about what he calls 'certain factions' – the PLO, President Gaddafi of Libya, Ayatollah Khomeini of Iran, the Muslim Brotherhood, and the Sunni fundamentalists, especially those of the extreme groups such as *Takfir wa'al Hijra* (Repentance and Holy Flight) and *Jihad* (Holy War). For various religious and political reasons all these 'factions' want to destabilise Egypt to the point of revolution. Mubarak has told his people, 'We must join together to combat the powers of darkness. Terrorism is as much a threat to majorities as to minorities, as much a threat to Islam as to Christianity.' Egypt's ten million Coptic Christians are *dhimmi* – second-class citizens – and they know they are one of the principal targets of the Muslim Brotherhood.

Military costs are formidable partly because hundreds of thousands of men must be maintained in the armed forces just to keep them employed and therefore politically passive. Mubarak has tightened Egypt's military pact with Sudan – the one Arab country which remained Egypt's friend after its peace treaty with Israel – and has diversified Egypt's weaponry.

Without Egypt, the strongest Arab nation, no general war against Israel has much chance of success. But Mubarak is aware, as was Sadat, that Egypt's economy was ruined by its wars with Israel. Despite difficulties, the country became much more stable after the peace treaty was signed in 1977. Mubarak works constantly at trying to repair relations with the Arab nations which broke with Egypt because of the treaty; he needs Arab investment to help with development plans. Vast amounts of money, much of it American, are being spent on development in the Sinai peninsula.

Egyptian society has one of the most definite class structures in the Middle East. At the top is the educated, almost aristocratic class which includes army officers; this group controls the nation. There is a large and wealthy merchant class and a very large class of minor bureaucrats, officials and clerks. Largest of all is the illiterate labouring class, the fellaheen of the fields and the slum-dwellers of the towns. Students are so numerous that they form a sub-class of their own, as do the sophisticated semi-Westernised Cairenes.

The Egyptian government encourages tourism and the country certainly has spectacular attractions for the tourist, from the pyramids and the sphinx to the Aswan High Dam. See MUBARAK: NASSER: SADAT: DEMOGRAPHY

ENMITIES

When the Arab world was a conglomeration of tribes there was always fighting in retaliation raids or in vindication of personal honour. Majid Khadduri[12] says that enmities 'stirred the deepest passions of the soul . . . the senseless and ceaseless tearing of faction against faction, with all its attendant violence to persons and property was restrained by nothing.' Enmity is deeply felt and an insult or an injury is rarely forgiven, though among urban Arabs the blood feud between families has practically disappeared. Peasant families in rural areas still feel it is their duty to avenge a murder or serious injury, especially if the offender belongs to an outside group. Both the accusing and the culpable parties are subject to court jurisdiction but in some circumstances the authorities decide to leave justice to the respective tribal chiefs.

It seems impossible for Arabs to forget an insult or injury, let alone forgive it and Iranians have the same attitude. The more extreme mullahs and imams teach that hatred is holy; ministers of education, notably in Syria, have ordered that hatred of Israel should be part of the school syllabus. Westerners are well advised to be careful not to offend people with whom they have dealings; they are not likely to be harmed but their business, whether economic or political, might well be terminated. See HATE: FANATICISM

ENTERTAINMENT _____

Visits between relatives, neighbours and friends are the main form of entertainment in the Middle East, even taking precedence over television-watching – though the two often proceed in tandem. People 'receive' not only at home but in their offices and shops. Any Westerner on business in Arab countries soon accepts that his meetings will be interrupted by people arriving unannounced. However important the business matter is, it is suspended while coffee is served and gossip takes over. I once spent an entire morning in a government office in Tripoli, Libya, but managed to get only 10 minutes' talk with the official I had called to see. People kept arriving and this meant another bout of hand-shaking and embracing bonhommie.

Besides the spontaneous occasions and the regular visits, there are special circumstances when a visit is obligatory, such as to call on somebody who has returned from a trip, or to greet a new arrival, or to pay respects in cases of sickness, death, weddings or family feasts. Omission of an obligatory visit is harshly criticised. Similarly, a failure to receive visitors, for whatever plausible reasons, is cause for severe reproach. The Arab, Sania Hamady[4] says, does not appreciate a perfunctory reception; 'he expects and enjoys a big-hearted and warm welcome.' The host – even if he is in his office and desperately busy – must not act as if he were in a hurry or indeed as if he had any other business at all. The visitor must be received with a smiling face regardless of the host's emotional mood – for the visitor might interpret gloom as directed against him.

The cinema is popular entertainment for all ages though young men predominate. It is not considered respectable for girls to visit cinemas with boys or young men. Men will sometimes visit three or four cinemas in a single day. Talking is a basic entertainment especially in country towns. Groups of men – never women – will talk for hours over coffee at a streetside café.

Being highly individualistic and concerned with self, Arabs are not great team players of any sport, though since the early 1970s high-priced European soccer coaches have been imported by the oil-rich countries in attempts to establish national teams. Tennis and swimming are popular among the moneyed classes and in the more cosmopolitan cities women are allowed to join in.

In Iran until the revolution of 1979 the young enjoyed the delights of discos and pop music but all this was banned by the mullahs as 'anathema to God'. Concerts in the Western fashion are almost non-existent, except in Israel; theatre, ballet and opera are also rare and nowhere, other than in the expensive hotels catering for foreigners, may men and women dance together.

Algiers, Tunis, Cairo, Alexandria, Beirut and Tel Aviv have their strip clubs and they can be found on Cyprus too but none would venture to advertise in neon lights in the European and American fashion. Cairo has some of the most sexually explicit night club acts in the world but officially they do not exist. Certain clubs in Cairo, Casablanca, Algiers and Beirut cater for the most perverted, degenerate and brutish of tastes. Until 1975 Beirut attracted wealthy men from all over the Arab world because it could offer the best and most bizarre in titillation. It is common knowledge that even in Saudi Arabia private sexual orgies take place between local men and foreign women, some of the girls being specially flown in for the occasion. Teheran also had its fleshpots but like most other 'imports from the decadent West' they vanished with the coming of the Islamic revolution.

FAHD, King

At the age of 62, Fahd became the fifth king of Saudi Arabia on the death of King Khalid, his half-brother, in June 1982. For some time, because of Khalid's ill-health, Fahd had been the single most important figure in shaping policy. In inter-Arab politics Fahd is a centrist, seeking consensus and trying to avoid Saudi Arabia's isolation. He is less anti-Egyptian than many Saudis and has been referred to as pro-American but this is a great oversimplification. He does, though, value Saudi's relationship with the USA and believes that Washington can be persuaded to support Saudi

Arabia without threats and confrontation. In his dealings with the West generally Fahd is often indirect, elusive and soft-spoken. Since King Faisal's assassination in 1975 the style of rule has become more collective, with several of the 5,000 princes having a say in government. Fahd is the fourth of King Abdul Aziz ibn Saud's 45 sons to come to the throne; 32 are still living and the youngest, Hamid, is 36. If Ibn Saud's strategy is followed to the letter then the throne could still be held by the same generation of princes in 30 years' time.

FAMILY

Duties and privileges within a family are sacred and compelling and the devotion of the family remains a moral and religious principle. To serve one's family is the first prerequisite for gaining approval. The minimum duty that a person has to fulfil is to serve and favour his kin.

In Arab and Iranian society formal respect is due to the father in the way others in the household speak to him and in the way they act in his presence. As the family's main contact with the world outside the home, the father is expected to be a forceful person and generous to the point of ostentation. This accounts for male display of personality projection and boastful bravado which can startle Western visitors to an Arab home. The Arab husband has few tasks in the home itself. The Arab mother is formally subordinate to her husband; her sole responsibility is rearing the young children and she functions as guardian of the household finances. She is expected to be frugal and industrious, unlike her husband.

Family life can be full of tensions, as Sania Hamady[1] explains: 'Serious conflicts inevitably arise from the communal life of an extended or tribal family in which a large number of people from various generational and collateral relationships live together. This is a fertile source of jealousy, hatred and defiance among the married brothers and their wives; the mothers transmit these feelings to their children. In general it is a life full of pain, bitterness and insecurity.'

The main cause of quarrels is an attack on one's family (or religion). Evaluation of a person's family and its comparison with others is constantly going on in the community. The family's reputation is highly important to its morale and its standing; consequently, the behaviour of its members in public is of special significance. The conduct of children during a visit or in the presence of guests, the food on the table, the rugs or furniture in the home – all are indices of family for others to observe.

In most parts of the Arab world family members are still held responsible for one another's conduct and for the punishment of those who do wrong.

In many cases a family is identified with a locality, owing to the frequency of marriage among cousins, the broad definition of 'family' to include distant relations, and the extreme care with which family connections are preserved. In a survey of a Lebanese village in 1975 it was found that of the 400 marriages over a century only 40 were with 'foreigners' from neighbouring towns; the vast majority were with cousins inside the large extended family.

In the Arab world the extended family is tied to the ownership and inheritance of land. A married man can own no land while his father lives so he remains part of his father's household. Inheritance of all forms of property among Muslims is governed by the detailed rules set out in the Koran (ch.4, verses 12ff), in the traditions of the Prophet and in intricate tales of family relationship based on these sources. A Muslim may freely dispose of only about a third of his property; the remainder must be distributed in accordance with Koranic prescriptions, which give no advantage to the oldest son. Sons inherit equally and each one twice as much as a daughter.

See CHILDREN: LAW: OBLIGATIONS: SOCIETY: WOMEN

FANATICISM

Fanaticism seems to be inevitable in societies which hold dogmatic religious and racial views and this applies throughout the Middle East. The traditional history of the region is full of sectarian violence, murder and massacre in the name of Allah. In modern times fanaticism has been most evident in Iran since the beginning of the Islamic Revolution inspired by Khomeini, in Sudan, Saudi Arabia and Lebanon. More generally it has been given violent expression by the Muslim Brotherhood, the PLO and other extreme groups.

It is entirely understandable in Islamic religious terms because Islam can admit no compromise with 'unbelievers, apostates and infidels.' As extremists and fundamentalists see it, these people, if they cannot be reformed or converted, must be killed. Christians are not immune to fanaticism; the men who carried out the massacres of Palestinians at Sabra and Shatila camps in Beirut in 1982 were Maronite Christians. Some Orthodox Jews in Israel are fanatics; they stone 'indecently dressed' women who venture into Orthodox communities, as well as car drivers on the Sabbath. Such fanaticism, however, does not lead to murder.

The attack on the Great Mosque of Mecca in Saudi Arabia in 1979 was carried out by Islamic fanatics, inspired by revolutionary mullahs and incited by Gaddafi. Fanaticism sometimes assumes hideous forms. For instance, the PLO terrorists who killed the Jordanian Prime Minister, El-Teb, on the steps of the Cairo Sheraton Hotel then licked up his blood.

See MASSACRES: TERRORISM: PALESTINE LIBERATION ORGAN-ISATION

FATE

Muslims are necessarily and inevitably fatalistic because of Koranic teaching. Perhaps the most frequently used phrase in Arabic is *In sha'a 'llah* (inshallah), meaning 'If God wills'. All that will happen in life has been laid down in the Koran, the Hadith and the Shari'a (q.v.) and no deviation is possible. Everything that happens was meant to happen – or *kismet* as the Arabs say. This does not necessarily mean in violent modern times that a Muslim will be passive and resigned on all occasions; if he appears to fight against fate then that too was meant to happen. But the average Arab has been leading a deprived and miserable life for ages and his fatalistic attitude is largely the result of a subsistence economy where people live in want until death. As Sania Hamady[4] observes, 'Being closely tied to his family and subjugated to severe public opinion, the individual survives by resigning himself to those external forces and accepts his lot as it comes to him.' As always, there are proverbs to express fatalism – 'Caution does not avert the decree of fate' and 'The provision for tomorrow belongs to tomorrow.' The Turks have a similar fate-related proverb: 'Destiny caresses the few and molests the many.' Hamady expresses all this more directly, 'Religious leaders have indoctrinated the people with a defeatist attitude to life, with unquestioning acceptance of authority and with resignation to their miserable lot in this world.'

FOOD

Pre-occupation with food in Arab society – as distinct from a natural interest in it – begins in infancy and extends through life. The essence of hospitality is the offering of food and in Islam, as in other Semitic religions, the food offering is sacred. But the Islamic attitude towards food comes from other influences as well – from endemic poverty and constant hunger, and from an unconscious seeking for the emotional security which social life fails to provide.

An Egyptian sociologist, H. Ammar,[13] notes Arab children's continual concern with food: they are nearly always eating or chewing something and their stories and teasing games usually deal with food. Adults, too, seem always to be chewing or drinking (and smoking) whether in company or not. The famous Egyptian writer, Taha Hussein,[14] is significantly revealing in his autobiographical story about a blind boy; he gives more attention to the boy's shame and embarrassment at his clumsiness while eating than to his inadequacy in running and playing with other children. Those Arabs who can afford to eat well consume large quantities of food. Their love of eating is revealed in a common proverb: 'When you eat you don't need to think.'

Sania Hamady[4] observes that 'food is the great medium

of satisfaction and a sign of succour and love.' The first sign
of affection shown by an Arab to a newcomer is to extend an
invitation to a meal or to send some special food to his
home. Most presents, Dr Hamady says, are in the form of
food and recipients are obliged to look upon the giver as
their creditor; they are expected to be grateful to those who
feed them. Two proverbs illustrate this feeling: 'The house
in which you eat, don't pray for its destruction' and 'Throw
no stones in the well from which you drink.'

Western visitors need to know that no matter how short
the visit, the guest is never allowed to leave before he is
offered some food and drink. If there are no provisions in
the house the host sends his child on a quick errand to buy
food – or to borrow it from a neighbour. If the guest declines
then the host will insist that he at least eat some sweet or
take a piece of fruit with him.

A guest arriving at mealtime is invited to eat and someone
will get up and offer him a place. The guest's first refusal is
a courtesy and he expects the invitation to be offered several
times before he yields. Then he is constantly pressed to eat
more and more. He often stops, pretending that he has had
enough while expecting the family will entice him to eat
more. To provide only enough food for a visitor is
considered mean; there should always be a surplus. On
arrival from a distance the guest is offered food whatever the
time of day or night; the wife will get up and cook especially
for him.

When a man invites several people to a big reception he
shows particular care in the presentation of the meal. He
carefully watches his guests' appetite and presses them to
honour him by eating a lot of his food. Sania Hamady notes
that his insistence 'almost amounts to menace'. Often the
host will not eat with his guests but will stand by to see that
each is amply supplied. He expects to be thanked effusively,
a wish which many Western visitors fail to fulfil, thus they
give offence. The wife – and any other women who may have
prepared or served the meal – should *not* be thanked, though
after the meal the host might call for his wife and publicly
thank her. Except in the more cosmopolitan circles of Cairo,
Tunis, Algiers and a few other cities the wife will not have

dined with the men, even when a foreign visitor is accompanied by his wife. In some places, such as Saudi Arabia, women and girls *never* eat with the men.

Special experiences are in store for those travellers who stay with bedouin. For instance the couscous-like stew into which all the men present dip their hands. The sheep's eyes are courteously left for the guest. More likely a roasted sheep will be brought in on a leather platter and around the sheep are steaming mounds of rice and flat loaves of hot bread. With fingers, the men tear chunks from the animal, dip it into the pool of fat in which it lies, and wrap it in a bread disc to eat it. A Western visitor is usually replete after minutes but bedouin men eat on for an hour before taking coffee.

In the traditional Israeli Jewish home every meal is a religious rite because it must be *kosher*, that is, prepared in accordance with God's commandments, as amplified and interpreted by rabbinical tradition. By Jewish law only certain kinds of meat and fish may be eaten. Orthodox Jews will only eat meat from animals that have been killed by a qualified *shochet*, a professional slaughterman working under religious supervision. A shochet prides himself on his skill and humaneness; this is important to Jews because they abhor cruelty to animals.

It is specially important that meat should have been drained of blood. The other great rule is that meat and milk must never be served at the same meal – a custom which Western visitors should remember. In an orthodox kitchen there are separate sets of utensils for meat and milk dishes, kept carefully apart. The best known food not permitted to Jews is pork. In the Reform tradition the dietary laws may be treated liberally or not followed at all. Most Israelis have a Western-type diet.

See ENTERTAINMENT: FAMILY: HONOUR

FRANCE IN THE MIDDLE EAST

As one of the two great imperial powers of the 19th and 20th centuries France has long been influential in the Middle East. Algeria, Morocco, Tunisia, Syria and Lebanon had

been either avowedly or tacitly part of the French empire.
Syria and Lebanon were held by Vichy (pro-Nazi) forces
during World War II until liberated by British
Commonwealth troops in 1941. In 1943 they became
independent. Finally France relinquished her hold on
Morocco, Algeria and Tunisia, though not without a
protracted, bitter and bloody war in Algeria. French business interests remain important, especially in the sale of
arms, in the former colonies and in Libya. French relationships with Israel have been uneven. With Britain and
Israel, France embarked on the Suez War of 1956 but later,
under de Gaulle, France refused to supply military aid to
Israel, even to the extent of breaking contracts. Having paid
for gunboats built at Cherbourg, Israel sent an undercover
naval party to 'steal' the impounded ships.

The French have been greatly troubled by Gaddafi's
operations against Chad (1976 – 1984) and other former
French colonies but late in 1984 Libya and France agreed to
withdraw their troops from Chad simultaneously; the
Libyans soon broke the agreement. The French have tried
unsuccessfully to bring about peace in Lebanon. Because
they see parts of the Middle East as within their 'sphere of
influence' the French remain important in the region but
French culture and language are more enduring than
French political and economic systems.

FRIENDSHIP

Several sociologists and psychologists have studied Middle
Eastern patterns of friendship and all agree with Sania
Hamady[4] that, paradoxically, friendship begins in a climate
of hostility. On initial contact each person is considered a
potential enemy so that they are 'tested' before they can
become friends. There is a proverb to justify this: 'Don't
make a friend of one whom you do not put to the test.'
When an Arab has carried out this test and found a positive
response he is a truthful and faithful friend.

Friends are sought on the basis of mutual aid, which is
not surprising in a society where so many people live at
subsistence level and where so many dangers exist. The

proverb 'The enemy of my enemy is my friend' influences Arabs from national leaders to fellaheen. Potentiality of help and reciprocity is a primary criterion for the selection of friends. Friendships become profound, with the exchange of complete confidence and allowance of little privacy. Yet, out of misunderstanding or envy, friendship can quickly turn to hatred and enmity, made even worse by the knowledge that the new enemy is in possession of all kinds of confidences. However, it seems that even in enmity confidences are often respected.

When an Arab or an Iranian offers friendship to a Western man he is generally sincere and he can be a very good friend indeed but it must always be remembered that he sees friendship as reciprocal; while he is prepared for demands to be made on his friendship he will make demands on his foreign friend.

Turks, Israelis and Cypriots are much more cautious in their friendship; it is slower to develop but once established is firm. Their friendship is less demonstrative than among Arabs and much less demanding. There is a quiet acceptance of reciprocity rather than a demand for it.

Friendship among women is rarely able to rise above the social level because women have little chance to meet other women outside the family. Women and girls are restricted to the home unless in the company of a male of the family and should a woman show real interest in another woman her menfolk would suspect it to be immoral or assume it to be a threat to themselves; that is, she would not be devoting enough time and attention to the men.

See GIFTS: HOSPITALITY: OBLIGATIONS: HATE

GADDAFI, President Muammar

Gaddafi came to power in Libya in 1969 after overthrowing King Idris in a bloodless coup. He was only 27 and one of the youngest of leading Arab revolutionaries. At first he ruled through a 12-man Revolutionary Command Council from which he appointed a prime minister but gradually his authority became more autocratic. A man of the desert, Gaddafi is something of a mystic and sees himself as the heir of President Nasser and therefore leader of the Arab nationalist movement. As a devout Muslim, he also regards himself as the Mahdi or 'expected one' who will sweep away the enemies of Islam.

Impatient and unpredictable, he has quarrelled with most Arab leaders and is hated by some of them. In particular he has earned the enmity of the Arab monarchs because he has urged their peoples to rise against them; Islam, he says with some justice, does not recognise kings and princes. He supports any cause which he conceives to be anti-imperialist and has therefore given help, money and training to many terrorist organisations, including the IRA, Baader-Meinhof (which became the Red Army Faction), the PLO, Black Panthers and the Italian Red Brigades. Many international terrorists, such as 'Carlos', and various foreign hijackers have found sanctuary in Libya.

At first Gaddafi was a benevolent despot for his own people but in reaction to attempted coups to overthrow him he has become more repressive; scores of his opponents have been executed for treason and for 'crimes against God'. Gaddafi has sent death squads to several European countries to kill dissident Libyans who have refused to return home; Libyans have been murdered in London, Paris, Rome, Lisbon, Madrid and Hamburg. In 1977 Gaddafi proclaimed Libya a Jamahiriya – a state run by the masses.

Also in 1977 Gaddafi produced his Third Universal Theory – his answer to the discredited systems of communism and capitalism – which works on the principle of committees everywhere to replace existing government administration. 'The problem of democracy in the world is finally solved,' Gaddafi announced. Throughout Libya posters proclaim that 'Parliaments are defunct', 'Parties are treason', 'The People are the Caliph, Law and President.' None of this means that Gaddafi has given up his authority and power.

Eager for an empire – as well as for Islamic supremacy – Gaddafi has either fought wars or engaged in subversive activities against Egypt, Sudan, Saudi Arabia, Tunisia, Algeria and Niger. The main threats to his life come from within the Arab world rather than from Israel, which he has sworn to destroy, or from the West. Since 1979 Gaddafi has financed the building of the Muslim nuclear bomb in Pakistan. During 1983 he engaged Carlos to give training courses to Libyan terrorist squads and then sent them to several countries to intimidate his enemies. Internally Libya is in a state of administrative chaos because Gaddafi dismissed civil servants and allowed 'the people' to take over.

See FANATICISM: LIBYA

GAMBLING

Koranic injunctions forbid all forms of gambling in Islam. There are two main references: 'In liquor and gambling lie serious vice as well as some benefits to mankind. Yet their vice is greater than their usefulness.' (Chapter 2: 219) 'Liquor and gambling, idols and raffles, are only a filthy work of Satan; avoid them so that you may prosper . . .' (Chaper 5: 90 – 91) Many wealthy Arabs gamble when abroad; in 1981 a London gambling club sued a Saudi prince for one million pounds in unpaid gambling debts. Little gambling takes place in the Muslim Middle East or Israel, Turkey and Cyprus.

GIFTS

The Western person must be cautious about giving presents in the Arab Middle East. In some countries and in some classes – such as the Egyptian upper class – it is customary to send flowers to one's hostess either before or after a party or to take a small gift. The best course is to ask about the local custom. In general, a man should not give a woman a present; her husband, father or brothers might accuse her of having incited the man to flirt with her. Similarly, a Western woman should never make a gift to an Arab man; he will almost certainly assume that she is expressing a sexual interest in him. Conversely, it is safe for a man to give a man a present, provided it is not too personal; a good quality pen is fairly safe. An American once presented a Syrian with a set of toilet preparations – and destroyed a relationship. The Syrian was insulted by what he saw as an implication that he *needed* to use soap and after-shave. Any kind of gift for a male child is acceptable but care is needed in selecting a present for a young girl; a plaything is acceptable, clothing is definitely not. Other than in cosmopolitan circles do not expect thanks for a gift; among Muslims it is accepted that the gift came from Allah and you are merely the vehicle by which it arrives. Gifts *from* Arabs are often expensive and ornate. I once asked President Gaddafi of Libya for a quite ordinary political poster of himself; it reached my hotel in a highly ornamental silver frame. His pride would not allow him to give me the poster in an envelope; I might think that he could not afford a good frame.

GOVERNMENT

The purpose of this entry is to describe the *organs* of government, rather than the *type* of government, which is covered under the entries Democracy and Dictatorship. Two major Middle East countries do not have a written constitution – Israel and Saudi Arabia. Israel has a British-type unwritten constitution based on tradition, parliamentary cabinet government and civil liberties; as in Britain the doctrine of separation of powers exists – the executive, the legislature and the judiciary are separate from one another. The case of Saudi Arabia is different; the ruler's will is supreme within the confines of Islamic law so no constitution is considered necessary. Revolutionary Iran is another exception because the constitution has been suspended by the present theocracy. In Turkey, too, parts of the constitution are in suspension under the emergency regime of General Evren.

The constitution of the Arab countries is 'flexible' in that rulers are able to modify it to suit their own policies at any given time. In Jordan, for instance, the constitution leads a precarious existence amid the realities of royal prerogative. Lebanon might also be considered an exception. It had a working constitution until 1975 but it collapsed under the turmoil of civil war and later of Syrian occupation.

Most countries do have a parliament and there is usually a form of cabinet but laws are more often made by decree than produced by debate. A vast administrative structure and complex bureaucratic procedure puts laws into effect. Much local administration is patterned on the French model with prefects appointed from the central Interior Ministry. The judiciary is not formally separated from the rest of the administration – as it is in democratic countries. Courts are part of the Ministry of Justice much as tax bureaus are part of the Ministry of Finance. Judges are in principle irremovable but punitive transfers to remote places and compulsory retirements limit their independence.

The armed forces under the chief-of-staff play an independent role within or *vis-a-vis* the government, even where they are supposedly subordinate to a civilian minister of defence. The armed forces have a *political* role, whereas in the democratic west they decidedly do not. The religious establishment is paid from public funds and except for Turkey, where secular legislation has been in effect since 1920, religious authorities still define and administer the law of marriages and inheritance; this includes Israel. Education is public and secular and its administration centralised.

Overall, the notorious instability and radicalism of Middle East politics are mitigated by a remarkable degree of administrative conservatism and continuity. The despotic type of government in the Arab Middle East may be criticised; the forms of government appear to work reasonably well but it must always be remembered that coercive law is predominant over administrative law.
See DEMOCRACY: DICTATORSHIP

GREETINGS

In Middle Eastern society greetings are ritualistic and formal, even when apparently informal. An order of priority according to situation, age and rank is observed in greeting – and in seating and serving. The single person must greet a group, the passer-by salutes the seated, the young man greets the older unless the younger man's position in society is higher. Any salutation must be answered; silence is interpreted as a strong indication of enmity or resentment.

As guests arrive a series of salutations begins. Women hold each other's right hand at length or bring it up to their lips as they make noises to simulate kisses on both cheeks. The young kiss the hands of elderly relatives and close relations. Men utter the phrase 'Peace be with you' while the visitor, bending slightly, passes his right hand in one gesture from his heart to lips to his forehead, thus indicating that his host is in his heart, speech and thoughts. Only friends shake hands and after long absences they may kiss each other on the head or shoulders. A Middle East man will accept a hand offered by a Westerner, even if they are meeting for the first time, but unless he is accustomed to Western ways he has to make an effort to do so.

At home, once the preliminary civilities are complete, the host embarks on further ritual – saying that the visitor has been sent by God, that he brings with him the sun and divine blessing, that he is a thousand times welcome . . . The guest employs similar ritual and will use some expression such as 'God multiply those who resemble you' or 'God recompense you.' A gesture, the right hand brought to the side of the heart, often accompanies an expression of thanks. Conversation starts by men asking about the children and families; they never ask about each other's wives, referring to them as 'your side' or 'your home'. At the end of a visit, friendly or ceremonious, elaborate phrases of thanks, compliments and good wishes are exchanged again between host and departing guests. In offices and shops greetings are much the same and take up a good deal of time.

In Iran greetings are similar to those in the Arab world except in largely Westernised Teheran, though since the Revolution the old customs are returning. In Turkey most educated people are similar to Western men and women in their greetings, while in Cyprus and Israel Western-type greetings are the norm. Elaborate ceremonial is out of place.
See HOSPITALITY: LANGUAGE

HADITH

In the last years of the Prophet Muhammad's life it was a pious custom that when two Muslims met one would ask for news (hadith) of the Prophet and the other would relate a saying or an anecdote. After his death the custom continued and the word hadith was applied to sayings and stories which were no longer new. In time an elaborate system of tradition was built up to supplement the Koran, which was found insufficient for the complicated needs of a rapidly expanding ideology.

During the first century of Islam – that is, to the middle of the 8th century AD – there were numerous living witnesses from whom traditions were collected, committed to memory and orally handed down. Every traditional memory consists of two parts: The text (matn) and the authority (sanad or isnad). For instance, the relater says, 'I was told by Ali, who was informed by Hassan, who had it from Ammar, that the Prophet – God bless him! – used to begin prayer with the words "Praise to God, the Lord of all creatures." '

This, then, became the practice for all Muslims. The forging of traditions became a recognised political and religious weapon. Even men of strict piety insisted that the end justified the forging of traditions. As a result of such elastic principles every new doctrine took the form of an apostolic hadith. When Bukhari drew up his collection of hadiths in 870 AD – he entitled it *The Genuine* – he limited it to about 7,000, selected from 600,000. The hadith are a profoundly important part of Islam.

See KORAN: ISLAM

HASHEMITES

The sect was founded by Abu Hashem, great-grandfather of Muhammad, in the 7th century and King Hussein of Jordan traces his descent from the Hashem family. The dynasty was in decline for centuries until the Turks, the imperial power in the 19th century, restored the Hashemites as puppet rulers. Britain took over the region after World War I and endorsed the Hashemite reign. Hashemites consider themselves entitled to high rank on the basis of being the Prophet's kinsmen, but the family was never respected in the more sophisticated parts of the Arab world, particularly among the nationalist Arabs of Palestine and Syria. King Abdullah, Hussein's grandfather, had dreams of a single Pan-Arab Hashemite kingdom stretching far beyond Jordan.

See HUSSEIN: JORDAN

HATE

Hate is inevitably a part of life in a society where people are sensitive about insult and slight, honour and dignity, pride and reputation, religion and politics. When a person does a serious injury to somebody the entire family of the wronged party will at once hate the entire family of the attacker and the hate can last for generations. Hate is a simple fact of Middle Eastern life, especially in religion; one sect detests another sect, the Maronite Christians of Lebanon and the Druze of Lebanon hate each other.

To what extent people hate is largely a matter of religious affiliation. Being more intense about Islam, the Shi'a Muslims are capable of greater hatred than the Sunnis. The Iranians have demonstrated their hatred for their own Bahi'a people, for the Egyptians, for the monarchists of the Arab world, and for the Americans, and for all 'enemies of the Revolution'. In personal life, too, hatred can be so intense that it warps a person's personality. A man most fiercely hates a person who causes him to be ridiculed. Muslims as a whole reserve their greatest hatred for the person who converts to Christianity or Judaism; he will be lucky to escape with his life.

Some hatred fairly quickly dissipates especially if recompense is made. In business it is possible to buy off hatred by arranging a good deal for the hater. It is often difficult to know if a man feels hatred because he may cover it up, especially if he is in the process of working out a way to gain revenge against the man he hates. The Westerner in doubt about a man's feelings should consult a third party. Arabs really *suffer* from hatred and it can consume them. Turks

also have fierce hatreds, though religion now plays little part in the list of causes. Nationally, their great hatred is the entire Greek nation. Reaction to hatred often takes the form of violence in Turkey. Outside the few cities where there is a Western influence Turks are clannish and tribalistic and hatreds pass from generation to generation. Among Jews hatred is not a general characteristic. It is notable that with a few bizarre exceptions the Israelis do not hate the Arabs and would, for many reasons, like to be friends with them. The Egyptians and Israelis who have met since their respective nations signed a peace treaty have liked one another.
See ENMITIES: FANATICISM: ISLAM: VENGEANCE

HOLY WAR

Muslims know this as *jihad* (sometimes spelled djihad) and the word means, literally, 'a great striving'. In general parlance it stands for holy war in the name of Islam. Jihad is a duty of Muslims and by Koranic edict it is directed against 'unbelievers' whether Christian, Jew or pagan. Constant and everlasting, jihad is nevertheless low-key except in times of crisis. Since 1945 crises have been frequent and jihad has been officially proclaimed on several occasions, notably by several Arab states against Israel in the wars of 1948 – 49 and 1973 and by Algeria in its war of independence against France, 1960 – 62. President Gaddafi frequently proclaims jihad against 'the imperialistic West'. In 1980 Saudi Arabia proclaimed jihad against Israel in the dispute over ownership of Jerusalem. In 1979 Ayatollah Khomeini embarked on jihad against the United States in particular and the West in general. Violent expression of his jihad can be seen in the suicide truck-bomb attacks against the American and French peace-keeping troops in Lebanon 1983. Khomeini and the Iranians also preach – and practice – jihad against Arab states 'guilty of crimes against Islam', such as Saudi Arabia. The crime is that the Saudis have a monarchy; Shi'as believe that monarchies should not exist in Islam. Conversion of 'unbelievers' to Islam is considered a form of jihad and it is much practised in black Africa.
See MARTYRDOM: PARADISE

HOME LIFE

Within the privacy of their homes the members of Arab and Iranian families have sharply defined roles and functions and patterns of behaviour. Nobody can ever be fully relaxed because it is necessary to anticipate visitors. The sitting room is never used by the family but reserved to seat and entertain visitors. Many items of its furnishings are used as symbols to indicate the standing of the family and are seldom used for their real purpose. For instance, illiterate homes will display books, poor homes will keep silver ornaments prominently exhibited and there will be many ornate mirrors in the homes of old people. Silverware, good dishes and soft linen are not used daily by the family but are put aside for the pleasure and comfort of the guest.

In families of comfortable means one bedroom is always set aside for guests even if this means that the family itself is cramped. Nobody sits still and silent for long in an Arab home because all are competing for attention. Girl children are constantly underfoot because they are forbidden to go away from the home. Nearly everything is common property except that which belongs to the father, whose word is law. Problems are rarely discussed by the family because this would imply that the father was incapable of making decisions. The mother, however, is in charge of the functioning of the household.

The pattern of Turkish family life among the ordinary people is very much the same as that of Arab families but there exists a large middle class with more advanced ideas of equality for family members.

In Israel there is a marked difference between the family life of those Israelis who came from Arab lands – the Oriental Jews – and the Western or European Israelis, the Ashkenazi. The Oriental Jews brought with them cultural attitudes and values, though women are now much more the equal of men and children play a full part in a shared family life. In most respects Israelis from Western backgrounds and those who were born in Israel have a family life very similar to that of Western Europe or the United States. However, many foreign visitors have commented that Israeli children are

pampered much more than those of European families.
See CHILDREN: FAMILY: WOMEN

HONOUR

Honour or *'ird* is so fundamental to the Middle Eastern
mind that Westerners must understand it if they are to
comprehend many Arab actions and attitudes. *'Ird* has
several variations, one of the most important being the
honour of the family. What other people think of a member
of the family, in both Arab and Iranian society, is
profoundly important. An advance from a man, even if the
woman has not encouraged it and is startled by it,
dishonours the family if the advance is observed or becomes
known to others. The greater the notice taken and the
greater the gossip then the greater the offence against *'ird*.

'Ird has another basic value. A Palestinian head of family
was asked to describe his feeling in leaving his village home
during the June War of 1967. 'We ran away with our
honour intact,' he said. (*Shirridna bi'irdna*.) The action to
which he refers involves both components of *'ird*: The
honour of the women and the response to physical
challenge. By the standards of *'ird*, he had responded
satisfactorily to the first component, saving the honour of
the women. But he failed to respond to the second, the
challenge of the occupying enemy army. To him, the first
component justified his action and took precedence over the
second. Honour of the women outweighed his honour as a
fighter. This priority of values is significant. A second point
is the use of the plural – '*We* ran away with our honour
intact.' This suggests that the honour in question is a
collective possession, something that belongs to more than
one individual.

The possibility of failure in any way fills the Arab and the
Iranian with dread, for this too leads to shame. Naturally,
such fear deters him from accepting responsibility. At every
opportunity, in conversation the Arab underlines his belief
that he has not failed; this is from president to peasant.
Again, his honour is such that he feels debased if he is pitied
and he does not easily ask for external help, as three much

quoted proverbs indicate: 'Die from starvation rather than ask for help,' 'Let my left hand not need my right hand,' and 'Better die with honour than live with humiliation.'

It is never wise to leave an Arab feeling dishonoured because he will not rest until the shame is expunged through retaliation. After the Israelis defeated the Egyptians and Syrians so resoundingly in the June 1967 War the Arab sense of shame festered. In the years following many Egyptians said wistfully, 'If only we could have a little victory.' After the better Arab performance in the 1973 war their sense of shame almost vanished, even though they did not win the war.

Turks have a much more matter-of-fact approach to honour except where the reputation of their women is concerned. Both Greek and Turkish Cypriots are sensitive about their honour though they quickly recover from real or imagined slights.

See LANGUAGE: VENGEANCE: ENMITIES

HOSPITALITY

Middle East standards of hospitality are set by long custom. They originated with the insecurity of the desert where it was a sacred duty to welcome and protect a passer-by; this obligation traditionally lasted three days. On departure the chief guest and host exchanged gifts for all the persons in each party.

In the towns and cities hospitality has a different function; as Morroe Berger[11] has observed, 'It reduces the tendency of the ever-present hostility to burst into violence at every moment. Exaggerated hospitality and politeness are reactions to exaggerated hostility.' The poorest nomadic Arab will kill the last animal he possesses to provide not just food but a banquet for a guest who may be a complete stranger. He is conscious of obeying a tradition set by his ancestors. A French writer, P. Dornier,[15] comments, 'In hospitality, as in everything else, the Arab carries his virtues to fantastic extremes.' A reputation for hospitality is valuable for any Arab, therefore he does all he can for a guest knowing that news of his generosity will spread. Many

Arabs are guided by the proverb, 'Generosity hides all defects.' The Arab aristocrat is a particularly generous host, at home or abroad; the lavishness of Arab parties is a talking point in wealthy circles.

Many Western people visiting the Middle East do not realise that hospitality must be accepted. To refuse a man's hospitality is to insult him by denying him the opportunity to display his qualities of character – notably generosity, good-fellowship and the ability to spend. Even when it is inconvenient the visitor is under compulsion to accept proffered hospitality because a refusal may lead to a counter-refusal. Whatever the reason for hospitality, it is still one of the Arab's most engaging personal qualities. It is equally evident in Turkey, though more subdued in presentation.

See FAMILY: OBLIGATIONS: FRIENDSHIP

HUMOUR

Few of the many people who have written about the Middle East have commented on humour, perhaps because they did not recognise humour when they saw it. Arab humour is very different from that in the West while Israeli humour is simply that of Jewish tradition. The fellaheen of the Upper Nile will laugh uproariously when somebody is knocked over by a donkey or falls flat on his face in an irrigation ditch. In cosmopolitan Alexandria the story of some sexual escapade will amuse people.

As Sania Hamady[4] says, 'the Arab is primarily and fundamentally a sad human being.' She makes the point that life comes hard to Arabs and they do not take it lightly. In any case, laughter detracts from one's composure. Women and old people, in particular, are supposed to observe the strict rules of reserve and restraint in laughter, in merry-making, in going to sports events – even in *feeling* light-hearted. Hamady claims that 'the Arab is not a good sport . . . he does not take jokes with grace.'

Frequently a playful situation can develop into a serious quarrel. It is never a good idea to 'play a trick' on an Arab or put him into a position, no matter how apparently trivial, where he might feel that he looks foolish in others' eyes. He would never forgive such a thing.

HUSSEIN, King of Jordan

Born on November 14, 1935, Hussein was the son of first cousins, both Hashemites. His father was Talal, son of King Abdullah, and his mother was Zein, a forceful woman with a keen political instinct. Educated first in Amman and then at Harrow, Hussein had an early introduction to the violent reality of Arab politics – his grandfather was murdered before his eyes. Talal was only briefly king before being pronounced insane; the throne passed to Hussein on August 12, 1952 when he was only 16 years of age and undergoing six months' military training at Sandhurst.

His first marriage was to Dina Abdul Hamed in April 1955 but the marriage lasted only 18 months. His second marriage, on May 25, 1961, was to an English girl, Toni Gardiner, who became Princess Muna. To the daughter from his first marriage, Hussein added four children from his second. Hussein's third wife, Queen Alia, was killed in an aircrash in Jordan in 1977 and in June 1979 he married an American, Elizabeth Halaby, aged 26, who converted to Islam and became Nur el Hussein, 'light of Hussein'.

Throughout his reign Hussein has performed a consummate balancing act in trying to remain friends with all the Arab leaders and with the West. His biggest challenge took place in 1970 – 71 during the Jordan Civil War, when the PLO terrorist leaders tried to turn Jordan into a PLO state. Because his Bedouin army was fiercely loyal to him, Hussein inflicted a bloody defeat on the PLO fighters and drove them from the country. Unable to resist his stronger Arab neighbours, Egypt and Syria, when they clamoured for war against Israel, Hussein lost the West Bank and East Jerusalem in the war of 1967. He stayed virtually aloof from the war of 1973.

At the beginning of his reign Hussein permitted a large degree of democracy but freedom bred instability as radical Palestinian groups and supporters of Hussein's bitter enemy, Egyptian President Gamal Nasser, sought to undermine his regime. Hussein ruled as absolute monarch but in 1984 he revived his long-suspended parliament, although having the power to suspend it at any time. He has survived at least 14 assassination attempts. Despite the dangers, he enjoys life and travels widely. A supreme pragmatist and a skilful politician, he has staved off military threats from Syria and Iraq and on the whole has enjoyed friendly relations with the West. Some observers say that his greatest skill is in never taking sides. He is by far the longest reigning ruler in the Middle East.

Members of three ethnic groups are in charge of security in Hussein's palaces. In Amman, the Bedouin soldiers of the Huweitat tribe are on guard around the clock. Circassian soldiers are responsible for security inside the palace while the servants are all black Africans. Highly trained security agents, some masquerading as maids, keep a constant watch on the staff.

See JORDAN

IRAN

Unlike most Middle East countries Iran has existed as a distinct culture and country for many centuries, since King Cyrus established a dynasty in 550 BC. The recent history of Iran has been dominated by the tremendous political

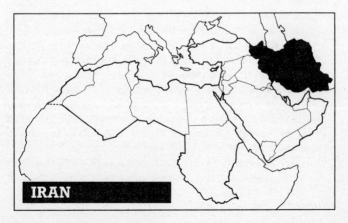

IRAN

conflicts of 1978 which led in 1979 to the overthrow and exile of the Shah and the creation of an Islamic republic under Ayatollah Ruholla Khomeini, aged 80. These events mark a historical turning point in Iran's history and they affect every aspect of the nation's life.

The revolution was largely the result of the Shah's policies, which, though often liberal and progressive, were oppressive. His secret police organisation, SAVAK, became notorious for brutality. The Shah under-estimated the power and influence of the *ulema* (religious establishment), which had financial backing from bazaar merchants and was able to mobilise large numbers of followers. Khomeini's government drew up a new Islamic constitution. This gives the ulema an important role in determining all legislation and ascribes great power to the president. It deprives the minorities of many rights, restricts press freedom and relegates women once again to an inferior role.

The Islamic Republican Party was made the only legal one, all opposition political movements were banned and the army was sent against the Kurdish rebels in the mountains. Thousands of former officials of the Shah's regime have been executed, as well as many people variously accused of being Zionists, 'enemies of God' and 'enemies of God's representative' (Khomeini). Between 1979 and 1985 2,400 women were executed for political reasons.

Under the Khomeini regime polygamy is again legal, men being allowed four full-time wives and as many temporary ones, or *sighas*, as they can afford. The minimum legal age for girls to marry was reduced to nine in 1980. Women are now barred from a number of professions, notably law, medicine and the teaching of male children. Men can divorce their wives when they please without even informing them. Iranian women have been most angered by the reintroduction of temporary marriages, which they see as an Islamic version of prostitution. There is no need to register such marriages and the men themselves can perform the necessary ceremony which consists merely of reciting a 15-word formula. Single women who refuse to become temporary wives risk prosecution for having an anti-Islamic attitude.

Early in the revolution Revolutionary Guards occupied the American Embassy (November 4, 1979) and held 52 staff hostage for a year. By overthrowing the United States' most heavily armed ally in the Gulf region, namely Iran under the Shah, and by encouraging fundamentalist militancy throughout the Islamic world, the Iranian revolution's leaders created many new problems further afield.

With a population of 36 million and oil revenues (in 1979 – 80) of 25 billion dollars, Iran has great regional importance militarily and economically. Foreign policy changed dramatically. Iran withdrew from the Western defence pact, CENTO, pulled its troops out of the province of Dhofar in Oman, broke economic links with Israel and South Africa, cancelled over 9 billion dollars' worth of defence contracts with the USA and expelled American military and intelligence personnel. Iran declared itself a member of the non-aligned movement and gave strong support to the PLO. Iran's relationship with the Soviet Union was almost as strained as that with the USA, which Khomeini labelled 'the great Satan'.

The drawn-out war against Iraq has deflected attention from much of the internal strife. It occupies an army that could otherwise become dangerously restless while achieving the removal of 'undesirables'.

In five weeks of 1983 – June 20 to July 29 – the authorities publicly announced 300 executions, mostly for political crimes, bringing the total since 1979 to about 40,000. Terror has led to counter-terror. In July 1981 Ayatollah Beheshti, Iran's second most powerful man, together with 150 other people, was killed by a bomb. Two months later the president, Muhammad Raja'i, and the Prime Minister, Muhammad Bahonar, were murdered.

In 1983 the purge against the Iranian Communist Party (the Tudeh party) and Soviet diplomats was further evidence of the paranoia that afflicts the Khomeini regime. The mullahs encourage army officers and government officials to spy on one another and create one special squad after another to eliminate officials suspected of anti-Khomeini plots. Major Mohammad Mansouri, an air force pilot who fled to Canada, claims that 'because of their medieval mentality and abysmal ignorance the mullahs feel intimidated by modern skills.' This has made them especially hostile towards the air force, and air force officers mysteriously vanish.

See KHOMEINI: ISLAMIC REVOLUTION: MARTYRDOM: SHI'A ISLAM

IRAQ

A Muslim country of 14 million people, Iraq has been ruled by President Saddam Hussein and a Revolutionary Command Council since July 1979. He inherited the presidency from the ailing Hasan al-Bakr and a few days later announced the discovery of a conspiracy against him. Within two weeks 21 Ba'athists were tried by a special court and executed; most had been close associates of Hussein. The episode appeared simply a device to enable the president to rid himself of potential opposition.

Power still lies with the Ba'ath Party; it recruits at all levels of the education system, down to primary schools. The party owes its position to the support of the armed forces which have gradually been purged of non-Ba'athist officers. Hussein's judicial murders did not improve Iraq's already lurid image in the outside world. The European public had been shocked by a series of assassinations and

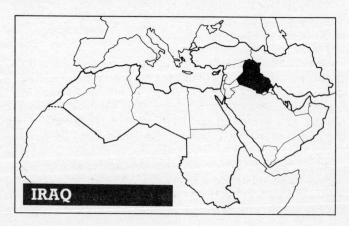

IRAQ

acts of violence by Iraqis in foreign capitals, particularly in
Paris and London in 1978. An Iraqi ex-Prime Minister was
murdered in London.

Over 90 per cent of Iraq's population are Muslims, with
the ruling Sunnis in a minority. Successive Iraqi governments have had serious problems with the nation's
1,500,000 Kurds, who demand independence. In 1975
armed Kurdish resistance temporarily collapsed when the
Shah of Iran closed his borders to the Kurds, thus depriving
them of a friendly base. Repressive methods made the
Kurds all the more militant and in 1978 the Iraqi army
burnt 650 Kurdish villages and deported 200,000 from the
north to the south. During 1979 many thousands of Kurds
and Communists were arrested, tortured and executed,
presumably in an effort to show the outside world that Iraq
is basically pan-Arab and anti-Communist.

Year after year Amnesty's *International Report* has
identified Iraq as having one of the worst records on human
rights in the world. A government official told a *Times*
correspondent, 'If you are an enemy of the revolution, if
you struggle against the revolution, then you will be
executed. People know what will happen to them if they
break the law. So it is perfectly fair.' Hussein himself, on a
BBC programme, said of people who oppose him, 'We have
got to cut off their necks' (sic).

In Arab-Israeli affairs Iraq has always taken an uncompromising posture, calling for the repudiation of UN
Resolutions 238 and 242 and for complete rejection of the
Israel-Egypt peace treaty. In June 1981 Israeli aircraft
bombed and destroyed Iraq's nuclear reactor, which the
Israeli government believed would be used to make nuclear
missiles for attacks against Israel. Hussein supports the
Palestinian splinter group led by Abu Nidal, which spe-
cialises in the assassination of PLO representatives (as a
reprisal because Nidal was expelled from the PLO) and
other men opposed to Iraqi policies.

Iraq had good relations with the USA until 1983 when the
Soviet Union offered to double any USA offer of money or
arms. The country's relations with its neighbours have been
complex and generally hostile, particularly with Syria.

Friendship with Iran ended when the Shah was overthrown. With Iran torn by revolution, Hussein went to war against it in mid-1980 to gain territory and oil. He expected a quick victory but the war dragged on with heavy casualties on both sides. Iran has sent revolutionary agents from Shi'a communities in several countries into Iraq to rouse the Shi'a masses to rise against the ruling Sunnis.

See IRAN: SAUDI ARABIA: ISLAMIC REVOLUTION

ISLAM

Linguistically, the word Islam means nothing more than submission (to the will of God) but the world knows Islam as the religious belief of Muslims. In fact, it is more than a religion; law, politics, economy and culture are all involved. Islam was founded – a Muslim would say 'revealed' – by the Prophet Muhammad in the 7th century. In 610 AD, at the age of 40 he began to preach the new faith which, he said, had been revealed to him by the Archangel Gabriel. In 622 Muhammad and a small group of followers travelled from Mecca to Medina; this migration became known as the *Hegira* and it marks the starting point of Islam. He and his successors spread the new faith by force and within a few centuries it was the dominant power in the Arabian continent, throughout North Africa and southern Spain.

Islam is based on the Koran, the *Sunna* and the *Shari'a*. Because of this basis, according to Professor H.A.R. Gibb,[16] the system is rigid, positive and emphatic. Nothing can be changed within Islam because the Koran was 'the final word of God'.

Almost from the beginning divisions appeared and they produced two major branches of Islam – Sunni and Shi'a. The Sunnis (or Sunnites) stress their adherence to the path (sunna) of the Prophet; they are the majority and the orthodox group. The Shi'as (Shi'ites) are the followers of the party (shi'a) of Ali, the son-in-law of the Prophet; they believe that Ali should have become caliph after Muhammad's death. The schism between the two has produced many bitter wars and insurrections.

Islam divides the world into only two parts – Dar al-Islam

(the land or region under Islam) and Dar al-Harb (the region of war, or that part of the world which must be brought under Islamic control).

The world's fastest growing religion, Islam is the official creed of 44 nations stretching from Morocco to Indonesia. It has at least 900 million followers and its leaders hope for 1,000 million by the year 2000. Islam is the complete way of life; perhaps this is its main attraction for the Christians and others who convert to it. It regulates property, marriage, divorce, family, punishment and justice, obligations, diet, sexual relationships, finance, race relations, war and peace treaties.

All Muslims owe five duties to Islam: prayer, fasting, struggle for the sake of Allah, commending good deeds and forbidding evil ones, and tithing. Islam's traditional ethics are also divided into five categories – things commanded, things commended, things deplored, things prohibited and a fifth 'miscellaneous' classification to deal with actions which do not fit easily into the other four.

Shi'a Islam is a religion of martyrdom as can be seen in Iranian cities during the Ashura ceremony, on the eve of the most important day of the month of mourning that begins the Muslim year. In Teheran particularly, hundreds of thousands of men parade through the streets reciting verses from the Koran and flailing their backs with zanjira – small iron chains. Their backs become ripped and bloody from the blows, struck to the rhythm of muffled drums. Many men also slice their shaven heads with scimitars as another token of their willingness to die for Islam. In 1983 Ayatollah Khomeini told the young men of Iran that Islam recognises only two amusements, shooting and horsemanship – because of their military value.

Saudi Arabia is the spiritual home of Islam if only because the holy city of Mecca lies within its borders and all Muslims should make at least one pilgrimage to Mecca. But Iranians owe as great an allegiancce to their own holy cities. Real power in Islam lies in the hands of the ayatollahs, imams and mullahs.

Western visitors to the Middle East should never initiate a discussion, let alone an argument, about Islam. At best,

Christians and Jews are regarded as misguided but in any case, in Muslim thinking, Islam cannot be discussed because it is absolute. Even the mildest criticism is offensive. Westerners must also realise that Muslims are not interested in *their* religion or creed. Dr Charles Malik,[17] a former prime minister of Lebanon and an ambassador to the UN expresses this succinctly:

> There is an amazing ignorance (in Islam) of Christian literature, doctrine and life, despite the fact that Christ and his Mother are revered by Islam. There isn't a single Muslim scholar in all history, so far as I know, who has written an authentic essay on Christianity; whereas Christian scholars, both Arab and non-Arab have written authoritative works on Islam and other religions too . . . There will always be fear, uncertainty, embarrassment, uneasiness, lack of joy, lack of freedom, and a predisposition to self-defence until this spiritual and intellectual imbalance is redressed.

Islam sees Jesus merely as a prophet of Islam. Unlike Christianity, Islam has no ordained priesthood hierarchy and the Muslim communicates directly with God, not through a minister. However, Muslim religious leaders, variously known as mullahs, imams and ayatollahs, have immense power and influence in religion, politics and law.

Equally, Muslims appear to attract the attention of the world's press. An American writer, Thomas W. Lippman,[18] has said, 'A casual reader of the daily newspapers could be forgiven for thinking that the word "Muslim" is an adjective used to explain violent events in remote parts of the world that are otherwise incomprehensible. "Muslim leftists" make war in Lebanon, "Muslim separatists" rebel in the Philippines, "Muslim insurgents" fight the Soviet Union's troops in Afghanistan, "Muslim militants" hold hostages in Iran, "Muslim extremists" assassinate officials in Syria, "Muslim cultists" make trouble in Nigeria.'

Muslims certainly make news even if the press sometimes gives them too much prominence.

See KORAN: MUHAMMAD: HADITH: LAW: SHI'A ISLAM: SUNNI ISLAM

ISLAMIC REVOLUTION

This is the name given to the movement which began in Iran with the overthrow of the Shah in 1979 and then spread beyond Iranian borders to the Arab world and beyond. Often called 'Khomeini's Revolution', the force of the movement lies in its demand for a return to the fundamentals of Islam. Its founders repeatedly state their opposition to Arab monarchs, Arab 'traitors' (such as President Sadat and President Mubarak of Egypt), Jews, the 'decadent West' especially the Americans, and enemies of the revolution, such as the inoffensive followers of the Baha'i faith. The aims of the revolution are to spread the word and power of Islam by every possible means, to restore Turkey as an Islamic state, to destroy Israel, to rid the Islamic world of 'pernicious' Western influence. Born in violence and bloodshed, the Islamic revolution continues in the same way and must be considered as perhaps the most dynamic force in the modern world. In effect, the Revolution is a 'return to the Dark Ages' as several observers have said, because it destroys the rights which Muslim women were beginning to enjoy, because it seeks to make Islam an enemy of the Christian West instead of a partner, and because it substitutes violence for negotiation and compromise.

See IRAN: ASSASSINS: TERRORISM: KHOMEINI: MARTYRDOM: SHI'A ISLAM: HOLY WAR

ISRAEL

Israel came into being as an expression of the long-standing desire of the Jewish people for a homeland; this desire became a craving during the Nazi period in Europe when six million Jews were slaughtered. Most of the survivors of European Jewry emigrated to Israel. The modern state of Israel dates from November 29, 1947 when the General Assembly of the United Nations accepted a recommendation from the UN Special Committee on Palestine to partition Palestine into independent Jewish and Arab states. From that time until the foundation of the state on May 14,

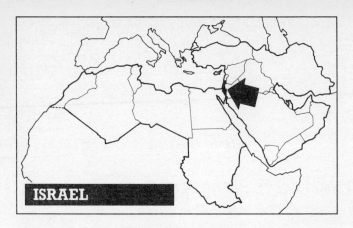

ISRAEL

1948 there was much Arab violence against Jewish communities and finally five Arab countries declared war. From that time until the present Israel has never known the luxury of permanent boundaries.

Roughly the size of Wales or the State of New Jersey, Israel takes up just one per cent of the Arab land mass. With an arid climate and limited natural resources – even water is scarce – Israel has nevertheless become a prosperous country with an economy based on tourism, agriculture and innumerable manufacturing industries. Despite the success of turning a basically unpromising and barren land into one of high productivity, every Israeli government has faced a massive budget deficit because of heavy defence expenditure. In effect, Israel has never lived without war but within this constant state of conflict several wars have occurred. They are: 1948 – 49 War of Independence; 1956 Sinai Campaign; 1967 Six-Day War; 1969 – 71 War of Attrition (mostly along the Suez Canal); 1973 Yom Kippur War; 1982 War Against the PLO in Lebanon. Throughout the state's existence a terrorist war has taken place against Israel, notably in the period 1967 – 82. Casualties have been heavy – almost 3,000 dead in the Yom Kippur war alone and more than 600 in 1982 – 85.

About 18 per cent of the Jewish population of Israel was born in Europe and the Americas, 16 per cent in Asia and

Africa and the rest are Israel-born, the Sabras. Nearly all the Oriental Jews were driven from the Arab lands and were taken into Israel as refugees. In addition there is an Arab population of 600,000 – the Israeli Arabs – and 80,000 Christians of 30 different denominations.

The only democracy in the Middle East, Israel has a Western-type single-chamber parliament (the Knesset) of 120 members, elected according to the list system of proportional representation, that is, each party has a list of candidates and those gaining the largest number of votes are elected to parliament. In effect, the entire country forms a single election district returning the 120 members, some of them Arab. This form of proportionalism leads to splintering of parties and the Knesset has had members of 19 parties, some with only one member. In 1984, 27 parties put forward candidates for elections. The life of each parliament is four years and parliament as a whole elects the President.

The leading socialist party is the Israel Labour Party. Mapam is the major socialist party to the left of Labour. The right-wing party is Herut (Freedom) and with the Liberal Party forms an alliance known as Likud. There are five religious parties – Shas, Morasha, Agudah, Masdal (the National Religious Party) and Tami.

Many of the pre-State Palestinian Jews lived on kibbutzim, that feature of Israeli life which has so captured the world's imagination. A kibbutz is a communal settlement where work is evenly shared and all property is held in common. Originally every kibbutz made its living from agriculture but now many industries thrive. The smallest kibbutz has only a few hundred members, the largest several thousand. Collectively kibbutzim hold only 110,000 of Israel's population of 4·4 million but they have produced a disproportionately large number of the nation's political, economic and military leaders. The 260 kibbutzim grow 40 per cent of Israel's agricultural produce which is 11 per cent of the GNP.

For many years Israel, as a small country constantly in danger of being overwhelmed by its enemies, attracted the world's sympathy and admiration. Arab propaganda and oil wealth then turned many countries against Israel, so that the country has been vilified in the United Nations. Israel had spent much time, energy and money in helping Third World nations. The peace treaty signed with Egypt in 1979 is regarded by most Israelis as the most important event in the nation's history, after independence.

The ever-present need to be ready to fight in the nation's defence has made Israeli soldiers probably the best in the world, though Israeli society as a whole regrets the need for compulsory military service. Israel is one of the few countries in the world where women are subject to compulsory military service, an indication of the nation's plight. Israel has much to offer any visitor; most Israelis are multi-lingual and the vast majority speak English. Road signs and most public notices are in Hebrew, Arabic and English. The holy places of Christianity, Islam and Judaism are open to all.

Yitzhak Shamir succeeded Menachim Begin as Prime Minister in 1983 and Shimon Peres became Prime Minister following the elections of 1984.

See JERUSALEM: JEWS: ZIONISM: FOOD

JERUSALEM _____

No issue is more delicate in the modern Middle East than claims of ownership and rights to Jerusalem. After the war of 1948 – 49 Jerusalem was a divided city, with Jordan holding the eastern sector and Israel the western. The Jews' holiest place, the Western or Wailing Wall, was within Jordanian territory. The Jordanians barred Jews from the Wall and gave Christians only limited access to their holy sites. During the 1967 war Israel captured East Jerusalem and unified the city which became the Israeli capital and seat of government. The Israelis found that the Jordanians had desecrated their holy places, nevertheless they opened the whole of Jerusalem to followers of Islam as well as to Christians. Because of Arab displeasure over Israeli control of Jerusalem nearly all nations maintain their embassy in Tel Aviv rather than in Jerusalem. The Israelis say that

Jerusalem is not negotiable and that no part of it will ever be returned to Arab control.

A beautiful city set among the hills of Judea, Jerusalem is an intriguing mixture of the ancient and modern and there is little to suggest that over the centuries 10 major battles have been fought for its possession.

The eternal significance of Jerusalem to Jews throughout the world can be seen in the thrice-daily prayer of observant Jews when they implore God to let them return to Jerusalem. Year after year, during the Passover festival, the prayer ends with the words, 'Next year – in Jerusalem!'

JEWS

Jews have inhabited the Middle East since ancient times. The occupying Romans expelled them from Judea and other parts of the Roman empire in the second century, though large numbers evaded the dragnet and stayed in Palestine. Those who were driven out formed the diaspora – the area of Jewish settlement outside the land of Israel – and settled in many places around the Mediterranean, throughout Arabia and in parts of North Africa. Clannish and intelligent people, they generally prospered despite periodic oppression. Though separated by religion from other inhabitants of the various countries, they were nevertheless loyal to their respective nations.

One of the great elemental Jewish values is study, expressed through the intense concentration on the study of sacred literature, the reverence for the scholar and the supreme stress on education. Another one of the most compelling of Jewish values is attachment to the Land of Israel, even during the many centuries when Jews were precluded from living in it. Nevertheless, many Oriental Jews had no real interest in travelling to the 'Jewish homeland' dreamt of by European Jews in the latter half of the 19th century. When the State of Israel was established in May 1948 they had no choice – with virtually no possessions they were driven out of every Arab country until only a handful were left in cities which once had large Jewish populations.

The refugees gravitated to Israel, their only sanctuary, where they started a new life. Some groups of Jews who preferred to remain in the Arab lands have been cruelly treated. The 4,000 Jews who stayed in Damascus are kept in a ghetto, where they live in poverty as possible hostages to be used against Israel. Those who stayed in Iran were equal citizens with Muslim Iranians until the coming of Ayatollah Khomeini as ruler. Most were forced out and some were executed as alleged spies.

See REFUGEES: JUDAISM: JERUSALEM: ISRAEL

JORDAN

An arid, oil-deprived, virtually landlocked country of 2·3 million inhabitants, Jordan has been central to Middle Eastern politics for 40 years. Modern Jordan is a recently contrived state with few natural boundaries and almost no tradition of nationalism. After the British captured Palestine from the Ottoman Empire in World War I they administered it as a League of Nations mandate; the territory east of the Jordan River, known as Transjordan, was put under Emir Abdullah. Becoming known as the Hashemite Kingdom of Jordan, the country left British control in 1946. The West Bank of the Jordan was not then

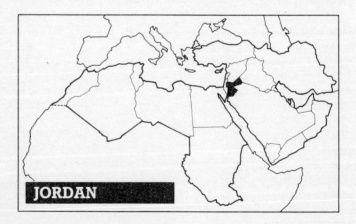

JORDAN

part of Jordan but Abdullah seized it, together with East Jerusalem, in 1950. The annexation was bitterly opposed by several members of the Arab League who saw it as expansionism by the Hashemite family.

Abdullah's move had profound consequences for Jordan; suddenly about 600,000 West Bank Palestinians were under Jordanian control. They, plus earlier Arab refugees, ultimately made the Palestinians the majority of Jordan's population. In contrast to every other Arab country, the Jordanian government offered the Palestinians full citizenship. The Palestinians, better educated and more industrious than Arabs east of the river, soon played an important part in the nation's economic, political and intellectual life. They filled important government posts, became the backbone of the civil service and they dominated banking and commerce.

Aided by its more favourable climate, the West Bank contributed 85 per cent of Jordan's agricultural output and 48 per cent of its industrial production by 1966. Thus it was a great loss in 1967 when Hussein pitted his army against Israel losing the West Bank. In 1970 Hussein nearly lost Jordan to the PLO, which was plotting a coup against him. Nevertheless, the great majority of Jordan's residents are Palestinian – possibly as many as 72 per cent – so it seems logical that the nation should eventually become the state which all Palestinians demand.

It is interesting that Jordan was the only Arab state to give unequivocal support to Iraq in its war against non-Arab Shi'a Iran; all the other Arab states fear the virulent, vengeful power of Shi'a minorities but apparently Hussein does not share this fear.

See HUSSEIN (KING): WEST BANK: PALESTINE LIBERATION ORGANISATION: ISRAEL

JUDAISM

Judaism is the religion of the Jews and it has been defined as the belief in a single all-powerful God with whom human beings can have contact, and the practical effect of this belief on people's lives. The basic prayer of Judaism, the

Sh'ma Yisrael, recited by the devout every morning and evening and attached in written form in a tiny scroll at the door of their homes, begins, 'Hear, O Israel, the Lord our God is one . . .'.

The most highly prized possession of the Jewish religion is the *Torah*, the first five books of the Old Testament, also known as the Pentateuch. The Torah contains what is believed to be God's revelation to Moses, and through him to the Jewish people, given on Mount Sinai over 3000 years ago. Many people, says ancient Jewish teaching, have had experience of God, but only Moses ever saw him face to face. The Torah contains 613 commandments ranging from the important, such as prohibition of murder, idolatry and the abuse of sex, to the apparently trivial, such as the instruction not to eat hare.

Judaism was not promulgated as an ordered system (as Islam was) and thousands of years passed before it was felt necessary to suggest a creed; there was, of course, a consensus of belief.

Judaism is not a mere intellectual conception or a dogmatic confession; it is a course of life lived under discipline. One of its cardinal principles is the belief in the Divine selection of the Jews to preach God's message. Despite this, in modern times the Jews are not missionaries and unlike Christians and Muslims they do not seek to convert others to their beliefs.

The English word *Judaism* derives from a similar Latin word which signified the Jewish quarter of a town or the Jewish community and it goes back to the name of Jacob's fourth son, Yehudhah or Judah, whose descendants were later called Yehudhim or Jews. Abraham is believed to have been the first adherent of Judaism. He is said to have reached the conclusion, through thought and revelation, that one Supreme God ruled the world and that idols were of no account.

Judaism is the religion of a minority – there are only 14 million Jews in the world – ever conscious of its duty to the majority by example and by martyrdom when necessary. Jewish and Christian conception of morals are identical but, while Christianity leaves much to the individual, Judaism sees a system of discipline as essential. The 'law' is important for Jews; for instance, no subject is more governed by law in Judaism than the Sabbath rest; it is regarded as the greatest boon among Jews and it is certainly so in modern Israel.

Modern Judaism has several forms, the most prominent being Orthodox, Conservative and Liberal or 'Reform'. Orthodox Judaism as seen in the Middle East is fundamentally ritualistic; it insists that the practices ordained in the Torah and amplified in the main body of Jewish law (the Talmud) are sacrosanct and binding. Conservative Judaism is a trend which developed in the USA in the 20th century which, while opposing extreme changes in traditional observances, permits certain modifications in rabbinic law to meet the changing needs of Jewish people. Reform (Liberal) Judaism is gaining ground because it is more pragmatic and less demanding in ritual and dogma.

In Israel supreme religious authority is vested in the Chief Rabbinate. It decides on interpretation of the Jewish law in cases which cannot be dealt with by the eight rabbinical courts, which have 65 officially appointed rabbis. Judaism has four holy cities; Jerusalem, Hebron, Tiberias and Safed, and 20 other Holy Places. Jerusalem is the most important because it is the site of the Western (or Wailing) Wall, the remaining part of the great Jewish temple of ancient times and the most important place of prayer in Judaism. Normal Jewish prayer is recited in the standing position; only on Yom Kippur (the Day of Atonement) do Jews kneel to pray.

A word much heard in relation to Judaism is 'Torah'. It is different from *the* Torah and is nothing more than the scroll used for reading in the synagogue and for the entire body of traditional Jewish teaching and literature.

Judaism has its zealots or fanatics. These people, who in Israel inhabit a few suburbs and towns as sole communities, are peaceful enough when left to themselves; they can become violent when they believe that holy law is not being obeyed. Orthodox men can always be recognised by the long corkscrew-curl of hair at each temple (and often by a heavy beard), their enveloping black garments and black hats with broad brim. In Orthodox families women always have their hair and legs covered.

See JEWS: JERUSALEM

KHOMEINI, Ayatollah Ruholla _____

Ayatollah Ruholla Khomeini, who brought down the Pahlavi dynasty of Iran and created the Iranian Revolution, has relatively shallow roots in Iran. His grandfather was born in Kashmir and his own father was born after the family moved west into Iran. Within Shi'a Islam, theological learning and authority are in the hands of the ayatollahs whose number is not fixed and who are not formally elected; they 'emerge' by the consent of their peers. Khomeini emerged in the 1950s but did not come to the notice of authority until the 1960s when he opposed the Shah's policies. Eventually he was deported and went to Paris where he lived and plotted. His loathing of the Pahlavi dynasty became remorseless and personal.

After he returned to Iran in triumph in 1979 – he was then aged 79 – he began a reign which has few equals in the whole of the Middle East history. Many of his sayings are well known.[19] Two examples:

> Every part of the body of a non-Muslim individual is impure, even the hair on his hand and his body hair, his nails, and all the secretions of his body.

> The person who governs the Muslim community must always have its interests at heart . . . This is why Islam has put many people to death – to safeguard the interests of the Muslim community. Islam has obliterated many tribes because they were sources of corruption and harmful to the welfare of Muslims.

See IRAN: ISLAMIC REVOLUTION: SHI'A ISLAM: FANATICISM

KINSHIP _____

This is profoundly important throughout the Middle East. The Arabs say of kinsfolk, 'Your relative, even if he chews you, will never swallow you.' Relatives are much attached to each other and are intertwined in a multitude of reciprocal rights and duties. The family consisting of parents and children is not the basic unit, as in the West; the joint family is of much greater significance. This larger family unit consists of the parents, their children, grandparents, uncles and aunts and all the collateral relatives.

Beyond this, the family is an extended group covering non-blood relationships and friends to whom kinship terms are given as an index of nearness, respect or love. Those terms given to non-relatives are mainly a sign of courtesy or an expression of affection and they do not carry the rights or obligations connected with blood relatives. Genealogy is a vital interest to Middle East people and one of the most satisfying compliments a man can receive is praise of his ancestors and relatives. Intermarriage adds to the cohesion of the family group. Mating is largely a family affair, but the basic social bond is the blood-tie of descent in the male line. The individual and his family never cease to have claims on each other.

See FAMILY: SOCIETY: TRIBES: OBLIGATIONS

KORAN[20]

The holy book of Islam, the Koran, was 'sent down' to the Prophet Muhammad through the Angel Gabriel. Islam's one 'miracle', the Koran is written in 114 suras or chapters and is about the length of the Christian *New Testament*. It is uncertain whether the whole text was recorded in writing in Muhammad's lifetime but Muslims regard it as the final and unchangeable revelation of the divine will, abrogating all previous records of revelation, such as the *Old* and *New Testaments*. The Koran speaks of the years before Allah's message to Muhammad as 'years of ignorance'.

The word *koran* means reading or reciting; in public recitation the Koran is intoned or chanted in slow melodic phrases, the correct art of which is taught in Muslim seminaries. The ideal is to know the entire Koran by heart. All the constitutions of the Arab countries are inspired by the Koran. In 1973 the Syrian Government wished to move away from this convention; the result was riots in the mosques and a revolt that was harshly suppressed.

Some scholarly Muslims believe that Muhammad was directly the author of the Koran and others suggest a Jewish source with Christian additions. It has links with Christianity and Judaism, though the commandments of the Koran are not absolute and have an escape clause. For instance, 'Do not kill any man, a deed God forbids, except for a rightful cause.' Koranic injunctions include:

> Do not pursue things you have no knowledge of.
> Do not falter or sue for peace; you will be the upper ones.
> Make war against those who believe not . . . even if they be People of the Book [that is, Christians and Jews] until they have willingly agreed to pay the *jizya* (tax) in recognition of their submissive state.
> Believers, do not make friends with any men other than your own people.

Numerous Koranic references refer to Christians as infidels; because they do not accept some of Muhammad's teaching they are 'people of low intelligence'.

Various English translations are available. The best are *The Koran Interpreted*, Arthur J. Arberry, (London: Oxford University Press, 1972) and *The Koran*, N.J. Dawood, (London: Penguin Classics, 1968).

See MUHAMMAD: ISLAM

KURDS

The Kurdish people, most of whom live in Iran, Iraq, Syria and Turkey, are an under-privileged minority in the Middle East. A fiercely independent Islamic people – numbering between 7 and 10 million – the Kurds have sought autonomy for many years but Arab and Iranian racism prevents them from getting it. In Iran, Kurdish fighters have been at war against Khomeini's troops since 1979; during 1983 15,000 fighters of the Iranian Kurdish Democratic Party and their Iraqi allies of the Patriotic Union of Kurdistan beat back an onslaught by 150,000 Iranian troops in what the Iranian

Army called Operation Dawn Three. Most Kurds do not raise the issue of a Greater Kurdistan; they are fighting only for democracy in their own countries. Hassan Ghazi, who set up a short-lived Kurdish republic in Iran in 1945 – 46, is still optimistic and claims that despite Khomeini's efforts to destroy them the Kurds control vast areas of Kurdistan with their own schools, hospitals and courts.

See IRAN: IRAQ

KUWAIT

At the north-eastern corner of the Arabian peninsula, Kuwait covers a mere 17,818 sq. km. and has a population of only 1·4 million but has probably the highest per capita income in the world. Its foundation dates back to 1756 and it is a constitutional monarchy under an Emir, Sheikh Jabir. In February 1981 Kuwait re-instated an elected parliament, the only directly elected body of its kind in the Persian Gulf. It has a strong Islamic contingent which has passed fundamentalist laws, for instance, banning consumption of alcohol by foreign diplomats.

Kuwait has a delicate religious and political balance. Kuwaitis comprise only 47 per cent of the population; Palestinians make up the next largest group, 20·5 per cent, and there are large numbers of Egyptians, Syrians, Iraqis,

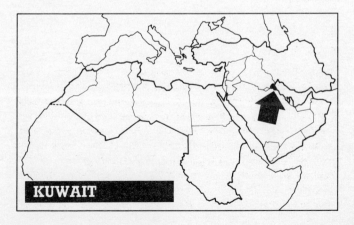

KUWAIT

Iranians, Indians and Pakistanis. A majority of the people are Sunni Muslim but an estimated 40 per cent are Shi'a Muslim, through whom Shi'a Iran has tried to foment unrest.

With oil reserves of 70 billion barrels, second only to Saudi Arabia in the Middle East, Kuwait is an attractive target for revolutionaries. Since 1964 Kuwait has provided much money for PLO funds as a form of 'insurance' against PLO subversion, the danger of which is great.

Vast amounts of petro-dollars are invested in the Western world, thus giving Europe and the United States sound reasons for wishing to protect Kuwait's stability. With well trained armed forces totalling 12,000 and loyal to Sheikh Jabir, Kuwait has some ability to protect itself and it can rely on the other members of the Gulf Co-operation Council. The publication of two English dailies, the *Arab Times* and the *Kuwait Times*, might give the impression of a pro-Western stance but of all the Gulf States Kuwait is least friendly towards the USA and it rejected Washington's nominee as ambassador. It is the only Gulf state to have diplomatic relations with Moscow and the only one to buy arms from the Soviet Union.

Six bombs were set off in Kuwait city on December 12, 1983 by the Islamic Jihad (Holy War) movement; these attacks were interpreted as a warning to the USA and France that their Middle East policies, in aiding Iraq, are unacceptable to the Shi'a Muslims, who support Iran.
See ISLAMIC REVOLUTION: TERRORISM

LANGUAGE

Albert Hourani,[21] one of the greatest Arab scholars living in the West, has said that Arabs are more conscious of their language than any people in the world. Language itself is an *act*; even more, by stating that something is so, it *is* so. This is a difficult concept for a Westerner to grasp but until he does so many Middle East actions and statements make little sense. For instance, in old Arabic the word *responsibility* and its concept were unknown. The word now exists but in modern life one is never responsible; it is always the other party who is to blame. Similarly, in general Middle East thinking, the victim is responsible for his own suffering. In the army an officer is not responsible and his men do not hold him so because authority carries no concomitant responsibility. When an Arab general commits suicide he does so from shame, not from a sense of guilt over his 'responsibility' for some debacle.

To understand the influence of language and literature it is necessary to go back to pre-Islamic days, for the beginnings of literary composition precede the art of writing. Poetry was always regarded as the model of inimitable excellence; the coming to light of a poet in the family was equivalent in importance to the birth of a boy or the foaling of a noble mare. The richness of the Arabic tongue has an almost bewitching effect on those who speak it as a native tongue. Naturally, oral communication assumes great importance in a society with high illiteracy. Poetry is today, as it was 1300 years ago, a part of everyday living. People improvise it by way of a pastime; versification appeals even to the illiterate, who usually know a certain number of famous verses. Arabic's wealth of synonyms provides for unrivalled possibilities in figurative speech, and with its depth Arabic can readily arouse passions.

Arabs have a talent for speech, an abundant verbal facility and skill in expressing a single idea under multiple forms. It should be remembered that the impact of words and forms counts more than the transmission of ideas, and there is much repetition in speech. An Arab word corresponding to a European concept must often be coined anew. Turkish and Persian absorb foreign words without difficulty but Arabic does not tolerate them. Abstract concepts are particularly difficult, for example socialism, communism, nationalism, reaction, freedom, state, nation, fatherland.

Israel's national language, Hebrew, has ancient roots but as a new language it was born in this century and is still growing to accommodate many new things and ideas. Educated Israelis are multi-lingual but all speak Hebrew among themselves. They share with the Arabs a love of poetry and many Israeli poets make a living from their craft.

A book of poetry will sell 30,000 copies, the highest number in the world in relation to the population.

Middle-Eastern Arab people speaking English or French as a second or third language try to make it work in the way that Arabic does. Thus, by Western standards, they speak in a flowery, fulsome and exaggerated way though this is less noticeable when they are in the West. It is a mistake for foreigners living in the Middle East or visiting there to try to match local rhetoric; the effect is forced and insincere and it can confuse those who are listening.

See BODY LANGUAGE: EDUCATION

LAW

In the entire Arab Middle East law is based on the Shari'a, the Islamic legal code. Most law is extracted from the Koran, and is often extended from it. The law differs from country to country depending on which of four major schools of interpretation – Hanafi, Maliki, Shafei and Hanbali – is followed. But in all schools judges opt for severity rather than leniency in case of doubt. Muslim jurists, in their various schools, accept basically the same views on fundamental dogmas and principles; they differ only in matters of detail and in the interpretation of cases.

Even when modern law is created by presidential or governmental edict it generally has a Koranic root. Law is revered because it is in the Koran and the commands of Allah govern all conduct. The exigencies of daily life have led to some change in formal law as administered by governments but the divine law remains virtually intact.

The new codes enacted by some Arab states are often influenced by commercial custom and by European patterns. No matter how complete the *Shari'a* might be it cannot hope to cover the complexities of the oil age. In Saudi Arabia, however, the only official legal system is Islamic law according to the Sunni Hanbali school. Saudi Arabia executed 63 men by beheading after they had taken part in the attack on the Great Mosque of Mecca in 1979.

Islamic legal doctrine does not operate on the basis of protecting the individual against the state; jurists subordinate the principle of individual liberty to that of public interest and welfare. For instance they concede the power of the ruler to employ the use of threats or the extortion of confessions by corporal punishment and imprisonment. Particularly harsh treatment is recommended for the individual of reputedly bad character whose guilt is suspected but cannot be proved.

Punishment is often summary. An American couple newly posted to Saudi Arabia caught their Pakistani houseboy stealing a few coins and ordered him to report to the police, expecting him to be reprimanded. They were appalled and astonished when he returned home minus a hand, the punishment for theft. It had been chopped off and the stub of his arm plunged into boiling tallow to disinfect it.

In recent years the mass media has revealed much about Islamic punishments, including execution of women for adultery, and flogging for drinking alcohol. General Zia al-Huq of Pakistan has said: 'The hard punishments of hand amputation and flogging are exemplary punishments for the good of mankind.'

Westerners should avoid situations which may bring them into contact with Middle Eastern law. This means not running foul of drinking regulations. Western people are generally permitted to drink alcohol in private but offering alcohol to Muslims is illegal. Many Westerners employed by contractors in Saudi Arabia have spent months and sometimes years in prison for 'corrupting' local people. Gambling is also prohibited and in revolutionary Iran is severely punished. In Kuwait even diplomats are not permitted to drink alcohol in private. Western companies and businessmen will inevitably have much to do with mercantile law in relation to contracts and the thousands of matters relating to them. No individual or company should attempt to do business in the Middle East without the help of a lawyer specialising in Islamic law. Reference books in English are scarce but I recommend *The General Principles of Saudi Arabian and Omani Company Laws: Statutes and Shari'a* by Nabil Saleh, published by Namara, London.

In Iran, before the Islamic Revolution, law was gradually

adapting to Western practice but that has all been swept away and replaced by a form of law which international lawyers are finding difficult to follow. Most foreign companies dealing with Iranian companies are arranging contracts *outside* Iran rather than venture into the complexities of Khomeini's law.

See KORAN: ISRAEL

LAWRENCE, T.E. (Lawrence of Arabia) 1888 – 1935 ___

Few Westerners are as much part of the Middle East as this British officer who during World War I was assigned to help the Arabs in the fight against the Turkish imperialists. An individualist, Lawrence appealed to the Arabs and he quickly adopted their garb and way of life. Partly through Lawrence's tutelage the Arabs defeated the Turks in the Hejaz; Lawrence's role in the overall victory against the Turks is over-estimated.

Through Lawrence's writings, and in what has been written about him, the Western world has received many of its impressions about Arabia and the Arabs. He painted a romantic picture of the nomadic Arabs with whom he lived and fought and one of his books, *The Seven Pillars of Wisdom*,[22] is a classic. Unfortunately his vision was limited, since it concerned only bedouin people, and it was romanticised, understandably so considering Lawrence's dependence on his Arab friends. Passionately loyal to these friends, Lawrence led Western readers of his books to expect too much from the Arabs, just as he gave the Arabs unrealistic expectations of the West.

LEBANON _____

The territory of the Republic of Lebanon, together with the Republic of Syria, the Kingdom of Jordan and the state of Israel belong to that part of Asia Minor which was known in the last century by the collective name 'Syria'. Going further back, the coastal region of Lebanon was Phoenician and pride in their Phoenician heritage is an essential element in the national consciousness of the present-day

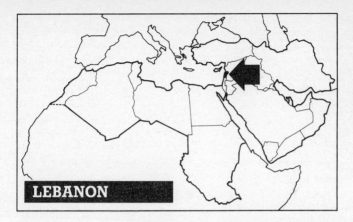

LEBANON

Lebanese. The country became independent from its imperial masters, the French, in 1941 and assumed the role of a republic in November 1943. Developing into a great banking and tourist centre, Lebanon became 'the Switzerland of the Middle East' in the 1960s.

The people belong to three major religions – Christianity, Islam and the Druze faith. The four most important Christian communities are the Maronites, Greek Orthodox, Greek Catholics and Orthodox Armenians. The Muslims are divided into Sunnis and Shi'as, with the latter in the majority. The Druze people are post-Islamic and live in communities in the Shouf Mountains. The Lebanese constitution, under the Lebanese National Pact, provides that the president is always a Maronite Christian – because Maronites were believed to be numerically preponderant – the Prime Minister is a Sunni Muslim and the Speaker of the Assembly a Shi'a. Lebanon thus became the only state in the history of the Arab world to realise equal co-existence between Christians and Muslims; it was also the only one in which members of parliament were democratically elected.

Before the Civil War of 1975 – 76 there were about 3 million Lebanese citizens together with a remarkable mixture of non-Lebanese residents. They included 500,000 Syrian 'guest-workers', Syrian Orthodox Christians from south-eastern Turkey, Kurds from Syria, Iraq and Turkey,

Christian refugees from Iraq, and political refugees from Syria, Jordan, Iraq and Egypt. The refugees most active politically were the 500,000 Palestinians. Eight major political parties and numerous smaller ones complicated the political scene, but despite crises, notably in 1958, Lebanon survived as a democracy.

The refusal of the Palestinians to obey Lebanese laws produced tension and conflict between Christians and the PLO and ignited an ongoing civil war. The PLO virtually 'owned' southern Lebanon and a large part was known as Fatahland, after Yassir Arafat's terrorist group. Syria, claiming that Lebanon is really part of Syria, invaded the country in 1976. Bitter factional fighting occurred and probably 100,000 people were killed between 1975 and 1982. Lebanon became ungovernable and its economy collapsed.

Because the PLO had been attacking its northern settlements for years, the Israeli Army in 1982 moved into Lebanon. The PLO was driven out and Lebanon and Israel signed a peace treaty but Syria refused to join.

All factions have been guilty of massacre; Muslims murdered Christians at Damour in 1976 and at Aachiya in 1977 and Christians massacred Palestinians in Beirut in 1982. In 1982 the newly elected president, Bashir Gemayel, was murdered. In October 1983, 241 American marines and 58 French paratroops of the peace-keeping force were massacred in truck-bomb attacks on their barracks in Beirut.

With the Iranians trying to recover Lebanon for Islam – they fear it will become a Christian-dominated state – with the superpowers striving for supremacy, and with the PLO trying to re-establish itself, Lebanon is unlikely to return to its pre-1975 peace and prosperity. It will not be a safe tourist country in the foreseeable future.

It is not possible to make sense of reports from Lebanon without understanding certain terms:

AMAL A Shi'a militia and political grouping led by Nabih Berry.

CAIRO AGREEMENT Signed in November 1969 between Lebanon and the PLO, the agreement defined the principles of Palestine residence in the country.

FREE LEBANON MOVEMENT   Maronite/Shi'a pro-Israel militia in southern Lebanon founded by Major Haddad, who died in 1983. It is now led by Major-General Lahad.

GUARDIANS OF THE CEDARS   An extreme Maronite group led by Etienne Saqr.

ISLAMIC AMAL   Breakaway faction of AMAL, led by Hussein Musawi and under the orders of Iranian Revolutionary Guards.

KATA'EB   Sometimes known as the Phalange, this is the largest of the Christian groups and most powerful political grouping; membership is predominantly Maronite. Its military wing is known as the Lebanese Forces.

LEBANESE ARAB ARMY   Founded in 1975 – 76 by Muslims who deserted from the Lebanese Army; pro-Syrian.

LEBANESE FRONT   Formed in 1976, the Lebanese Front is a group of rightist parties mainly Christian.

LEBANESE NATIONAL MOVEMENT   Formed in 1969, LNM is a loose coalition of mainly Muslim groups.

LEBANESE NATIONALIST FRONT   Comprises Syrian Social Nationalist Party, the Lebanese branch of the Syrian Ba'ath and the Union of Popular Working Forces.

MARADA BRIGADES (or ZGHORTA LIBERATION ARMY)   Pro-Syrian Maronite militia.

AL-MURABITUN   Mainly Sunni militia and active in Beirut.

NATIONAL LIBERAL PARTY   Mainly Maronite party with some Shi'a and Sunni members, the NLP's militia was crushed by the Kata'eb in 1980.

PROGRESSIVE SOCIALIST PARTY   Druze military and political organisation under Walid Jumblatt.

See CHRISTIANS (MARONITES): DRUZE: PALESTINE LIBERATION ORGANISATION: TERRORISM: FANATICISM

LIBYA

A vast country of 1,759,540 sq. km., Libya has a population of only 2,700,000, plus perhaps half a million guest workers. The majority of Libyans are Arabs but there are Berber villages in the south and west. An Italian colony from 1911, Libya was liberated by British and American armies in 1943 and was formally proclaimed an independent monarchy in December 1951, with King Idris on the throne. On September 1, 1969, when the king was abroad, a group of young army officers under Colonel Muammar Gaddafi, from Fezzan, seized power. An ardent admirer of Egypt's President Nasser, Gaddafi put forward his ideology in the three volumes of his *Green Book*.

The sole political organisation, the Arab Socialist Union, formed in 1971, was never effective, being overtaken by the local 'popular committee' system, which elects members to the General People's Congress. Gaddafi states that any form of government other than congresses of the whole population is undemocratic; Libya, he insists, is a *jamahiriya* (a state of the masses) and not a *jumhuriya* (a republic). Prosperous because of vast oil revenues, Libya has a high per capita income. It also has probably the highest per capita military spending, with more tanks, ships and aircraft than trained men to crew them. Libya channels large sums of money into the faltering economies

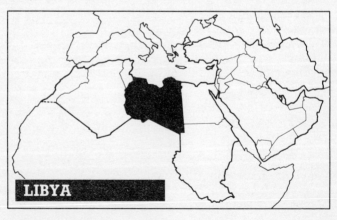

LIBYA

of Turkey, Greece and Italy, the leading suppliers of goods for the Libyan market. The Libyan Arab Foreign Bank has a 415 million dollar stake in the Italian car company, Fiat.

Libya's relations with its immediate Arab and African neighbours are governed by Gaddafi's ambition to be leader of the Arab Muslim world with the result that despite his many appeals for Arab unity, Libya has frequent direct confrontations with other Arab states. On the Palestinian issue, Libya opposes any compromise with Israel and takes the lead in uniting other hardliners – Syria, Algeria, South Yemen and the PLO – under the banner of 'steadfastness front'.

Libya has much to offer the tourist in Roman and Greek antiquities and some of its coastal and desert scenery is striking. Potential visitors need to inquire about the current state of Libya's foreign policy – is it violently anti-American or anti-British? – when planning a tour. Businessmen cannot expect to negotiate a contract or complete a project quickly; bureaucracy is all powerful.

Large numbers of students are employed by the Libyan Intelligence Service to report on foreign visitors. The usual ploy is for a student to strike up a conversation with a visitor and invite him to a café for coffee. He will later submit a report containing every detail of the conversation. This activity is mostly harmless but foreigners do need to understand that a file is started and that little is missed; the volume of Libyan files on foreigners is vast. Most Arab countries have street signs in Latin characters as well as Arabic script; Gaddafi ordered all Latin signs removed so visitors often have difficulty in finding their way about. See GADDAFI

LOVE AND SEX

In a similar book about other regions it might be possible to distinguish between the two but this cannot apply in the Middle East, other than among those communities with strong European or Western influence. Love is frequently a subject in Arabic and Persian poetry but generally in the physical sense rather than in an abstract way. While Arab and Persian peoples feel 'love' as other races do their culture has given it a different form of expression; from the male point of view it is fundamentally overwhelmingly possessive while the female is slavishly submissive. A strict code forbids discussion of sex between men and women, even between husbands and wives. Nevertheless, it is a common topic among men and among women when men are not present.

The code of sexual behaviour is so strict and restraining that whenever an Arab or Persian man finds himself alone with a woman he makes sexual approaches to her. In public any demonstration of love is frowned upon and Arab men often try to show the opposite to love. Hamady[4] says, 'He does not try to pretend indifference towards the object of his affection but shows hatred, negative criticism and ridicule . . .' A proverb sums up the male attitude: 'If you hear him swear at her know that he loves her.'

Sexual relationships are dominated by male impulses. Arab men place great value on their sexual prowess. They boast of their virility, which they like to flaunt – hence early marriage, the taking of more than one wife, and easy divorce. Many children are a tangible proof of a man's virility. Patai[23] says that, 'Virility is one of those overriding qualities which a man will uphold even if he must in the process sacrifice other values. Any aspersion cast upon virility is considered such a great dishonour that a man will make extreme efforts to remove every shadow of a doubt about it, even at the price of taking the onus of other dishonours upon himself.'

Impotence in a husband is one of the few causes for divorce which can be claimed by a wife. Should this allegation be true the husband will usually consent to a quiet divorce so as not to be exposed to the shame of publicity. If it is untrue – a woman may make the allegation maliciously – his sense of honour is deeply wounded and he will insist on proving potency even though this may mean performance of the sexual act before witnesses. Reports are vague about how exactly this is arranged but it involves the use by the couple of what is termed a *bayt al-shan'a* (house of abomination). This is a tent in which one or more respectable people can see and hear what is going on between husband and wife. The neighbours' observations and conclusions decide the fate of the marriage.

In Iran love cannot exist because the new regime makes women little better than breeding machines for Islam's warriors-to-be. Sex itself has no psychic dimension; it takes place for a man to impregnate a woman or to satisfy his lust with a 'temporary wife'. A woman may not refuse such an arrangement without running the risk of being tried by a religious court. In Iran, as elsewhere in Islam, it has long been said that a man should have intercourse with 'a woman for a son, with a goat for relief and with a boy for pleasure.' This is not to deny the pleasures of union with a woman but mutilated as she so often is – by 'female circumcision' – she cannot provide the satisfaction of a young boy.

The word 'joyful' is often applied to sexual relationships in the Western world but it does not fit Middle East society, because there is no equality of pleasure. A wife dare not show pleasure for fear of being considered a voluptuary; Middle Eastern men assume that only courtesans are voluptuous.

One of the saddest results of male pre-occupation with sex is 'female circumcision', so much a feature of life in some Middle East countries. Millions of girls and women have had their external genitalia removed, sewn up or infibulated – fastened with a clasp or buckle. The instruments used are razor blades, knives, fingernails, pieces of broken bottle, slivers of flint and thorns of the dwarf acacia tree. The 'mildest' form of mutilation consists in slicing off the tip of the clitoris with a sharp instrument. This practice is recommended by a number of Islamic authorities under the name 'Sunna circumcision'. The World Health Organisation believes that 30 million women from the Yemens, Saudi Arabia, Iraq, Jordan, Syria and southern Algeria have had the whole of the clitoris as well as the inner lips excised. The most radical form of mutilation is infibulation, which the Sudanese call 'Pharaonic circumcision' and the Egyptians 'Sudanese circumcision'. After the removal of the clitoris and inner lips the labia majora is sewn together – after scraping to ensure that they will stick together.

The basic reason for all this is that men consider that women have a hypersexual nature which must be controlled. Men are also supposed to have more pleasure with excised or infibulated women, though this idea has no medical basis.

As in other matters, the Koran provides directions for men about their relationship with women, including sexual activity. 'You shall not wed pagan women . . . A believing slave girl is better than an idolatress, although she may please you . . . Keep aloof from women during their menstrual periods . . . Then have intercourse with them as Allah enjoined you. Women are your fields; go then into your fields as you please . . .'

Homosexuality is more prevalent in the Middle East than in the West because of strict segregation of the sexes. Various surveys have shown that most males have homo-sexual relationships during the teenage and young manhood periods. In many Middle Eastern hotels the youthful male staff make it very clear by look and gesture to male guests that they are available.

Most Israelis see love and sex in Western terms. In sexual matters Judaism advocates moderation but distrusts total abstention, except during a woman's menstruation and for seven days after. In the past some Jewish sects, such as the Essenes, have advocated celibacy but mainstream Jewish teaching stresses the value of married and family life. There is a positive commandment for men to procreate. Religiously speaking a Jewish bachelor is almost a contradiction in terms. Divorce is regarded as a tragedy and as a failure in a central part of Jewish life.

See MARRIAGE: HONOUR: WOMEN: DESIRES

MANNERS

Middle Eastern people appreciate those who respect their traditions and manners. The Arab befriends easily those who understand his way of life and spare him humiliation. Preserving appearances is a primary concern among Arab people – and no less so among Iranians and Turks. Traditional wisdom is full of proverbs and sayings urging people to guard 'appearances', especially in front of neighbours and enemies, and this is why the Arab is often consciously hiding his poverty and unhappiness.

Arabs have excellent manners. They are affable, cordial, welcoming and helpful and all these characteristics naturally impress foreign visitors. But these good manners are deceptive in three ways. The Arab promises more than he can fulfil; he may suddenly change from composure to loss of control; he has a special kind of personal diplomacy which is a mixture of blandishment and adulation. An American observer, W.E. Hocking,[24] notes that Arab 'charm is not based on illusion, for the Arab has great virtues and equally great graces. But the deception lies in what you can depend on. Try to do something with the man who offers you coffee and puts his whole estate at your disposal! You will be maddened by his incapacity to resolve, to begin, to find means to the end, to carry on, and to finish. He is full of competent words but he tackles nothing . . .'

MARONITES

See CHRISTIANS

MARRIAGE

From selection of a mate to the contract and consummation of marriage, family functions are much more important and much more in evidence than in the West. Marriage is virtually compulsory and when a boy or girl reaches marriageable age – 16 to 20 for daughters and 18 to 25 for sons – the parents look to their relations and friends for a proper match. Quite often pairs of parents – or more likely pairs of fathers – have agreed years before that their children will marry at the appropriate time. In the cities a girl will generally be consulted but she is expected to defer to the wish of her father and brothers. In some communities marriages are contracted at birth and consummated at puberty; girls are often given in marriage to much older men.

When parents agree on a match the bridegroom or his father pays a bride-price to the wife while her parents pledge the amount of her dowry. A Muslim marriage is not a sacrament but a contract, although there is nothing in it to prevent polygamy or repudiation. The only religious content is that the contract itself begins with the traditional, 'In the name of God, the compassionate, the merciful,' and the parties recite the opening verse of the Koran. The contract is signed in the presence of a Muslim official authorised by religious and civil law. The groom signs too but the bride's consent is given by her father, brother or some other male relative. The contract is binding although the marriage is not yet consummated. The wedding ceremony itself takes place a few days or a few months later.

Separate feasts and entertainments are enjoyed at the home of the bride's parents and at that of the groom's. Bride, parents and relatives make an elaborate procession to the groom's house, carrying the goods they are contributing. Here another ceremony takes place, after which the couple occupy the part of the house reserved for them. From the moment of marriage the man considers the woman his property or possession and it is her duty to obey him in all things.

A Saudi Arabian girl trained in the USA as a radiologist observed, 'The Arab male does not want a marriage partner, but a possession over which he has total ownership. And if you try to convince him that a genuine partnership would be a much better relationship he becomes afraid for his dominance and falls back on religion as evidence for his supreme authority.'

Marriage in Israel is an elaborate ritual but much depends on just how orthodox the participants are. Among Orthodox Jews the ceremony is formal and colourful and full of vitality, with energetic dancing. A kibbutz wedding is a gala occasion; never again will boy or girl be at the centre of so much attention. Convention, usually so irrelevant on a kibbutz, comes into play and the bride acquires a wedding dress, veil, special shoes and the day before the wedding she

visits a hairdresser and beautician. The religious ceremony
is not taken very seriously; it is a mere duty to the state. The
wedding feast is much more important.
See LOVE AND SEX: WOMEN: HONOUR

MARTYRDOM

Martyrdom is a fundamental part of Islam, especially for
Shi'a Muslims for whom it has a long tradition. To die in
the name of Islam brings paradise as a reward. In modern
times the world has been astonished by the willingness of
some Middle East Muslims, notably Iranian Shi'as, to die in
the name of something they regard as a great cause. The
men who rammed their truck-bombs into American and
French bases in Beirut and died in the ensuing blast
illustrate this very well. In killing Christian 'imperialist'
soldiers whom their ayatollahs had declared to be enemies of
God they were dying for Islam. Many terrorist or resistance
groups include the word martyr in their title – Heroic
Martyrs of Haifa, Martyrs of the Return, Martyrs of the 6th
of June. The very use of the word implies a willingness to
die. The intensity of Shi'a devotions produces more martyrs
than does Sunni practice. The assassins of President Sadat
saw themselves as martyrs ridding the world of a 'traitor to
Islam'.
See SHI'A ISLAM: ASSASSINS: PARADISE: FANATICISM

MASSACRES

The world has become more aware of massacre in the
Middle East following the orgy of killing carried out by
Phalangists against Palestinians in the camps of Shatilla and
Sabra, Beirut, in 1982. The estimated number of victims
was 2,000. Because these events were given so much graphic
coverage by the mass media many Westerners formed the
impression that they were unique. In fact, massacre is
commonplace.
   In 1860 the Druze massacred 12,000 Christians in the
Shouf Mountains, Lebanon. In 1970 Sudanese troops
massacred 30,000 members of the Ansar sect on an island in

the Nile. In February 1982 7,000 Syrian troops, on government instructions, carried out massacres in the city of Hama. Amnesty International believes that deaths could have totalled 20,000; 70 civilians were shot outside the municipal hospital. The inhabitants of apartment blocks were killed by cyanide gas pumped into the buildings floor by floor. The victims were paying the penalty for 'anti-government activities'.

Frequent massacres have taken place in Iraq since 1979 and both Iraqi and Iranian troops massacred enemy civilians during the war of 1980 – 85. During the Lebanese civil war massacres were committed by Phalangists, the PLO, Shi'a and Sunni groups. Since 1960 massacres have been reported – and mostly confirmed – in nearly all Middle Eastern states, including Cyprus and Turkey.

MECCA

This city in Saudi Arabia is the holiest place of Islam. Muhammad lived here when he received the word of God and here too was built the Great Mosque of Islam. The city is forbidden to non-Muslims and special police ensure that none get through the control points. Muslims are expected to make the *hajj* or pilgrimage to Mecca at least once in their lifetime and each year more than two million people make the visit. The traditional time for the *hajj* is in the month of *Thil-Hijjah*, the twelfth lunar month of the Muslim calendar; on the tenth day of the month the blessed feast of *al-Adhha* (the sacrifice) takes place. Most of the visitors live in tents on the plains of Arafat near Mecca for a week of ritual of feast and prayer. Thousands of sacrificial sheep and goats have their throats cut in sacrifice. In 1979 revolutionaries paid by Gaddafi tried to take over the mosque by force as part of a plan to bring down the royal house of Saud. Hundreds of people were killed before the attackers were captured and beheaded. Iranians plotted to seize the mosque in 1983 but were forestalled.

See PILGRIMAGE: ISLAM: SAUDI ARABIA

MODERNISATION

Developing communications, technology, industry, banking systems and means of travel have brought profound social changes to the Middle East. Change has been so great since 1960 that people have not been able to adapt to new ways of life and of living, with consequent tensions and confusion. The greater part of the Middle East was still 'backward' before 1960, even primitive in many places. Rapid industrialisation meant that countries did not have enough trained people for factories, petrotechnology, hospitals and offices. This resulted in large numbers of foreigners being brought in to do the work. Because they brought with them ideas and customs alien to the Middle Eastern way of life the conservative regimes have been alarmed.

The Iranian Revolution is, in part, a rebellion against modernisation. While happy enough to use Western appliances, tools and methods, Middle East people are still confused by the changes they have brought. Perhaps most disturbing of all has been the focus of mass media attention given to the Middle East. Much of it has been critical and some of it hostile. Middle East governments and peoples are well aware of the criticisms and they resent it. This is understandable because the Koran tells them that they are the best of people and the most favoured. Many foreigners expect Arabs to 'modernise' according to Western terms. Even *attempts* to modernise produce some startling effects. The civic authorities of Jedda, Saudi Arabia, built north-south and east-west flyovers to keep traffic out of the crowded streets. The concept was excellent but the engineers did not build the two roads over-and-under; the result was that these two highways in the sky met at traffic lights!

MOROCCO

With a population of nearly 25 million, Morocco is the second most populous Arab nation, after Egypt. It is also one of the largest, covering 458,730 sq. km. It is overwhelmingly Sunni Muslim with very small minorities of

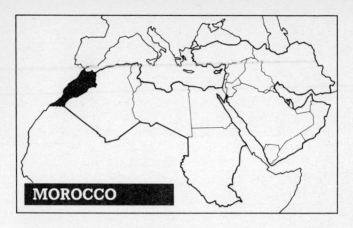

MOROCCO

Christians and Jews. Morocco has a Chamber of Representatives and a variety of political parties but power is concentrated in the hands of the king, Hassan II, who came to the throne in 1961. The 1972 constitution allows the king to dissolve parliament and to rule by decree.

The annexation with Mauretania of the former Spanish colony of Western Sahara is Hassan's greatest asset and greatest liability. He faces an apparently endless war against the Polisario Front, the guerrilla group backed by Algeria and Libya, over the ownership of the region, which is barren but phosphate-rich. The war has produced a jingoistic unity and pro-royal nationalism. But the cost has been great – an economic decline which threatens the downfall of a monarchy uneasily sandwiched between democratic Europe and the radical regimes of Algeria and Libya. In 1984 defence spending was more than 2,200 million dollars, an immense proportion of the national budget, and the inevitable result of keeping a third of the army on double pay in the Sahara.

Inflation is rampant and the nation has foreign debts of 8,000 million dollars. 70 per cent of all Moroccans live almost at subsistence level in a countryside where 3 per cent of the population owns 33 per cent of the land. The bottom fifth of the population, growing at an annual rate of 3 per cent, absorbs only 7 per cent of the national income; the top fifth absorbs 65 per cent. Unemployment ranges from 15 per cent in the cities to 50 per cent in the rural areas. With the nation's essential phosphate exports static in price and volume the statistics indicate the potential for social upheaval.

The USA, following its humiliation in Iran, turned Morocco into a symbol of America's renewed willingness to stand by beleaguered friends. Military aid rose from 30 million dollars at the end of the Carter term to 50 million in the first year of the Reagan administration; for 1985 the figure will be 185 million. While Morocco is undoubtedly a valuable American military ally, its importance should not overshadow other important considerations. The military access and transit facilities granted to the USA cannot be used against countries friendly to Morocco. In addition, King Hassan's ability to support American initiatives in the Middle East is constrained by his dependence on Saudi Arabian money.

Dissent simmers just beneath the surface and occasionally violence erupts; in 1983 General Ahmad Dlimi, Hassan's strongest army supporter, was murdered. The Moroccan armed forces have a rebellious tradition and there is ever present danger of a military coup. Hassan has survived several assassination attempts. The government arrests and often tortures uncompromising opponents of the monarchy, Marxists and fundamentalist Muslims. In 1984 Amnesty International estimated that Moroccan gaols held 1,100 political prisoners. More and more of the country's 120,000 university students – 25,000 are already studying in France – are tempted to go into exile.

MONARCHY

See GOVERNMENT: DICTATORSHIP: names of individual kings and princes such as HUSSEIN, HASSAN, FAHD

MUBARAK, President Husni

Mubarak, an air force officer, came to power in Egypt in October 1981 after the assassination of President Sadat.

Many feared that he would reverse Sadat's peace initiative with Israel but he honoured the treaty. He also followed Sadat in maintaining friendly relations with the USA. Much less charismatic than Sadat and Nasser, Mubarak is probably more pragmatic than either of his predecessors and he has steadily worked at rebuilding the Arab world's confidence in Egypt.

After Sadat's murder Mubarak dealt firmly with the Muslim fanatics without seeming to be vengeful. Like Sadat, he will not permit religious-based political parties, but they exist underground. Some militants approve of Mubarak's campaign against corruption, his curbing of luxury imports and his studiously private family life, but they have not forgiven him for endorsing Sadat's peace with Israel. He is no less a target for assassins than Sadat was. Mubarak is well aware that some of the Egyptians' frustrations and tensions are the result of the policies of the two previous presidents. 'Nasser made promises and Sadat fed expectations,' he has said.

See EGYPT

MUHAMMAD

Muhammad was born into the respected Meccan clan of Hashim about the year 570 AD. Orphaned at the age of six, Muhammad was brought up first by his grandfather and then by an uncle. As a youth he listened to Christians and Jews arguing over their faiths. At 25 he accepted a proposal of marriage from Khadijah, a rich Meccan widow 15 years his senior, for whom he worked as a caravan leader.

A mystic, Muhammad spent six months in solitary meditation at Mount Hira, where the Angel Gabriel progressively revealed God's word to him. The year was 610 and Muhammad was 40. He began to preach the new faith of Islam and was expelled from Mecca because his new beliefs threatened the town's tolerant Christian, Jewish and pagan religious atmosphere. In 622 he and a group of followers fled to Medina, 200 miles from Mecca. Gaining authority and power, he came into conflict with the Jews he sought to convert. Then he marched against the unbelievers at Mecca, captured the town and turned it into Islam's holy city. Muhammad retained the Christian and Jewish idea of a holy day but made it Friday, the day on which he reached Kuba, near Medina, the scene of his first success.

While married to Khadijah, Muhammad took no other wife but he was married 11 times in all, mostly to divorcees and widows. His sons died in infancy but four daughters survived. His daughter Fatima married his cousin, Ali, and had two sons. Shi'a Islam grew from this family.

Militarily Muhammad was ruthless and at least once he condoned massacre. Politically he was an opportunist, seeking alliances wherever possible. When Muhammad died in 632 Islam was a flickering light illuminating only a small part of Arabia. After his death it grew into a political-military-religious force which conquered much of the then known world.

See ISLAM: MECCA: PILGRIMAGE: RAMADAN: KORAN

NASSER, President Gamal Abdul _____

Born in 1918 Nasser was one of the few genuinely charismatic leaders of the 20th century and his role in arousing Arab nationalism cannot be overstressed. As a young Egyptian Army officer during World War II, Nasser was often in trouble with the occupying British. As a colonel, he was the brains behind the overthrow by General Naguib of the Egyptian king, Farouk, in 1952. Nasser soon replaced Naguib and he ruled virtually as a dictator from 1954. During the period from 1956 to the time of his death in September 1970 he was the world's most famous Arab, as befitted a man who had become the first Egyptian ruler of his country since the time of Alexander the Great.

Nasser achieved great prestige because of the Anglo-French failure to capture the Suez Canal in 1956. In 1967 he suffered a tremendous military defeat at the hands of the Israelis during the Six-Day War but his accumulated prestige enabled him to survive. His mistakes were spectacular – the abortive union with Syria, the bloody and protracted war in Yemen – but he was successful enough to make himself into a model for aspiring Arab leaders, Gaddafi for instance. Nasser was detested by some Western leaders, such as Anthony Eden, but in foreign policy he was generally a moderate man other than in his obsession to destroy Israel. He made the Egyptians a proud people through powerful oratory and by building up a huge army and air force. He promised his people so much so frequently that they imagined they had a higher standard of living than was really the case. His weaknesses and failings, now so widely recognised, do not seem to have reduced the masses' love for him.

See EGYPT: MUBARAK: SADAT

NATIONALISM

This is the over-riding sentiment among Arabs though it is equally strong, in a more limited geographic sense, among Iranians, Turks, Israelis, Greek Cypriots and Turkish Cypriots. One of the greatest movements of the 20th century, nationalism is more than anything else the mood which has impelled some Arab countries – and Iran since 1979 – to expel every trace of foreign influence and to strive for economic and military growth. In a way nationalism began as an effort to create a new self-conception for the Arab, a new identity. For centuries, Middle East people seemed to the West to be narrow, indolent, violent and unstable; so pervasive was this view that even Arabs came to accept it. Nationalism has changed the Arab's self-image and the world's conception of him.

While the first nationalist goal was to get rid of the imperialists other goals extended from it, so that solidarity – President Nasser's word – among Arab states was a major target. Beyond that was a desire to play a major part in world politics, an ambition which became feasible through massive oil wealth. Nationalism, then, had a negative side – rejection of political ties with the West – and a positive side in the building of national strength. Over a period of half a century Arab nationalism, 1920 – 1970, drifted from traditional liberalism to political extremism.

Arab writers frequently sing the praises of Arab nationalism. Other forms of nationalism, they say, are transitional but Arab nationalism is 'eternal' and has 'an eternal mission to mankind – because it is universal, democratic, progressive, revolutionary, positive and active.'

A modern Egyptian writer, Darwish al-Jundi,[25] says that the Arabic language is the strongest foundation of Arab nationalism. 'It has drawn together the Arabs and has been the means of communication of both their mind and spirit since the emergence of Islam.' Indeed, the West should never forget the strong Islamic thread within Arab nationalism. Even the most pragmatic, moderate and pro-Western Arab leaders have at times woven Islamic beliefs and exhortations into their policies and utterances. Gaddafi does this constantly.

Nationalism has a rather different emphasis for Iranians, Turks, Israelis and Cypriots of both Turkish and Greek origin. When they refer to nationalism they are merely speaking of a single, strong and independent nation – their own. It is a natural enough form of chauvinism. Arabs, in contrast, are speaking of a force which spans and links nations. 'Arab nationalism' is rather like 'Arab unity' in that it is a goal which cannot be reached because of rivalries and even hatreds among nations. The few attempts to unite nations in the spirit of Arab nationalism – for example, Egypt and Syria and later Egypt and Libya – have failed disastrously. Nevertheless, Arab nationalism has succeeded in giving Arabs a greater awareness of themselves in a world role.

See CIVIL WARS: DEMOCRACY: DICTATORSHIP: GOVERNMENT

NESTORIANS

See CHRISTIANS

OBLIGATIONS

Obligations are profoundly important in the Middle East and while they are most noticeable among families they extend to groups. For instance, group members are obliged to buy from one another's shops, to refer legal matters and medical problems to lawyers or doctors within the group.

Preferential treatment is expected, as well as a lower fee or price. Mutual expectations cover many fields, to lend money, food, clothing and anything else needed. Other obligations are to stand by each other in case of factional troubles and to repay visits.

Arabs often say in a ritualistic way, 'Please don't be grateful, you will repay me.' This sums up the sense of pervading obligation. Should a person fail to fulfil an obligation a simple and prompt excuse is not accepted. The explanation must be elaborate and convincing and it is often offered in a pleading manner. Enmity can result if an individual cannot provide adequate reason for failing to meet an obligation. Western people need to be aware that by Middle East tradition they are obliged to repay, in one way or another, whatever their Arab or Iranian friends have given them or have done for them.

See ENMITIES: FAMILY: HOSPITALITY

OIL

Oil wealth had no impact on Middle East politics until the 1960s. Up to that time it had made individual Middle East families wealthy but it was not considered a national asset and it did not provide a better standard of living for the Arab and Iranian masses. In any case, the larger part of the profits from oil went to the great Western oil companies. Gradually, the Arab countries – influenced by spreading nationalism – became aware that oil was their property and they demanded a greater profit from its exploitation. They also saw that it was unrealistically cheap and demanded higher prices.

Oil did not become a 'weapon' until 1973 when the Middle East oil-producing countries increased prices fourfold, just before the Egyptian-Syrian attack on Israel that year. Towards the end of that war the oil countries threatened to withhold oil from those European countries which supported Israel. It was this crisis which demonstrated to Western governments their vulnerability to political pressures applied through oil.

Following the fourfold price rise the Arab countries

became immensely wealthy and they invested their profits in the West. These 'petrodollar' investments are so vast that should a major Arab country, such as Saudi Arabia, withdraw its deposits from any one Western country, its economy would probably collapse. In 1983 the proven oil reserves of the Middle East accounted for 54·4 per cent of the world's total. The West has reduced its consumption considerably, though the average OPEC export price continued to rise until early 1981, when it reached a peak. The price was substantially reduced in early 1983. Because oil will account for a decreasing proportion of the West's energy requirements it is no longer such a powerful 'weapon' but it still provides the money needed for the Arabs and Iranians to finance their vast armaments purchases. More critically, it is the need for Persian Gulf oil which involves the United States and other Western nations in military and naval operations designed to keep the area stable.

See references to various countries, e.g.: SAUDI ARABIA: LIBYA

OMAN

With a population of less than a million, Oman is oil-rich but owes its stability to the strength of its ruler, Sultan Qaboos bin Said. He is Prime Minister, Minister of Defence

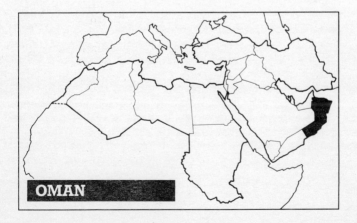

OMAN

and Minister of Foreign Affairs and the 22-member cabinet is firmly under his control. The majority of Omanis are Ibadhi Muslims; about 25 per cent are Sunni, with a smaller number of Shi'as. There are large numbers of migrant workers, including non-Omani Arabs, Baluchis, Pakistanis and Indians as well as British and Americans.

Oman is a member of the Gulf Co-operative Council, with Saudi Arabia, Kuwait, Bahrain, Qatar and the United Arab Emirates. In the politically disturbed environment of the Gulf the strategic importance of the Straits of Hormuz, through which passes 60 per cent of oil of the non-communist world, is a major issue. Financial assistance for Oman's defence has been guaranteed by other Gulf Council members, as well as military aid. (The state was known until 1970 as Muscat and Oman.)

OTTOMAN EMPIRE

The Ottomans began their history in the 13th century as a Turkish warrior tribe on the Anatolian border of the Byzantine empire. Their conquests spread spectacularly and took in much of the Arab Middle East. At their zenith the Ottomans controlled the most powerful – and the last – of the great Muslim empires. The military elite of the Ottoman Empire, the Janissaries, were originally drawn from among Christian boys levied as tribute from Balkan subjects; for several centuries they were forbidden to marry so that they could not be tempted to promote the sons of a marriage union or to build up ambitious families. Most of the Ottoman grand viziers were predominantly non-Turkish and even non-Muslim in background. The Ottoman Empire came to an end as a result of World War I; the British fought the Turks in Palestine, Syria, Mesopotamia (Iraq), Persia (Iran) and eventually defeated them. The peace treaties gave all the former Ottoman territories either to Britain or France.

See TURKEY

PALESTINE LIBERATION ORGANISATION (PLO) __

The PLO is the 'umbrella' organisation of a number of Palestinian groups, variously labelled terrorists, commandos or guerrillas. It came into being in 1964, largely at the instigation of President Nasser, as a political tool for the development of Arab nationalism.

At first supported by money from the Arab oil states, the PLO embarked on a dual-strand policy of terrorism and propaganda against Israel and its supporters. The number of groups affiliated to it has varied but the most prominent are Fatah, The Popular Front for the Liberation of Palestine, the Popular Front General Command, the Arab Liberation Front and Sa'ika; up to 40 groups have been affiliated at particular times. Fatah, the group controlled by Yasser Arafat, was always the most powerful though some of the most atrocious terrorist acts have been carried out by the PFLP (George Habash) and PDFLP (Nayef Hawatmeh).

Intrigue and violence within the PLO have led to many murders but the PLO managed to preserve the appearance of a respectable political body. In 1970 King Hussein of Jordan, fearing that the PLO was plotting to take over his country, bloodily expelled the various factions in a 'civil war'. While the basis of the PLO's wealth was oil money, it amassed vast reserves through a world-wide Palestinian head tax, through drug trafficking, extortion, ransom and bonuses. President Gaddaffi paid the PLO group Black September 5 million dollars in 1972. The PLO had £1,000 million invested in European and American banks in 1982.

Recognised by many countries as the 'legitimate voice of the Palestinian people', the PLO has set up offices in 110 of the world's major cities. Yasser Arafat was permitted to speak to the United Nations General Assembly in 1974 and in 1982 he was received in private audience by the Pope. The PLO had always been prominent in Lebanon but after 1970 Beirut became its main headquarters and the base for an elaborate military and quasi-political structure. From Lebanon, terrorist groups made hundreds of raids into Israel, attacking buses, homes, kibbutzim, hotels and schools.

In June 1982 the Israelis launched their 'Operation Peace for Galilee' to drive the PLO out of southern Lebanon. This aim was achieved and the PLO withdrew from Beirut. In 1983 Arafat's leadership was challenged by Syrian-backed PLO dissidents. The PLO's operations were curtailed by the 1982 war but the organisation and its constituent groups were by no means destroyed; backed by the Soviet bloc and by Syria, Libya, Algeria, Iraq and Yemen – and still wealthy – it had an assured future, though not necessarily with Arafat as its leader. Abu Musa leads the Syrian-backed portion of the PLO.

See ARAFAT: TERRORISM: LEBANON: WEST BANK

PARADISE

For Muslims, paradise is very much a real place and the hope of reaching it profoundly affects Islamic attitudes and actions. In several chapters of the Koran the paradise awaiting believers – and the hell for unbelievers – is vividly described. A comprehension of the joys of this paradise is necessary for any non-Muslim wishing to understand how Islam inspires its followers. As described in Ch. 56 of the Koran, *That Which is Coming*, paradise is a delightful garden, 'the Abode of Peace,' the abiding mansion where the worthy dwell forever by flowing rivers. Here they praise Allah, recline on silken, jewelled lounges, and enjoy heavenly food and drink in the company of dark-eyed maidens of perfect chastity and purity. Virtuous men recline on couches raised on high in the shade of thornless sidrahs and clusters of banana palms, amid gushing waters and abundant fruits, unforbidden, never-ending.

This most perfect of places is only for those who have fought for Allah, those who have suffered for Him, and are godfearing, humble, charitable and forgiving. The early Assassins, when embarking on a murder mission, had no fear of death because they were promised paradise. In modern times PLO and Iranian terrorists have been imbued with the same belief. Ayatollah Khomeini's Shi'a suicide battalions have gone into action against the Iraqi army inspired by the early expectation of reaching paradise. The drivers of the truck bombs which killed American, French and Israeli troops in Lebanon in 1983 – 85 committed suicide on the same basis. It is interesting to note that the Koran does not specifically promise paradise for women, though there is obviously an acceptance of the 'dark-eyed houris'.

See MARTYRS: ASSASSINATION: HOLY WAR

PEACE

The Middle East has never known peace. War, rebellion, civil war, insurrection and insurgence have been commonplace for centuries and never more so than in the 20th century. Paradoxically, many people of the Middle East *want* peace and the area as a whole *needs* peace if it is to develop educationally, economically, agriculturally and socially. Peace is fragile because of nationalistic aspirations, Arab and Persian pride and sensitivity, inter-Islamic hatreds, hostility towards Israel, border disputes, terrorism, religious rivalries and political or dynastic power struggles. Even if Israel were to achieve its desire to be at peace with the Arab world a general peace is not foreseeable.

The Koran offers no general advice about the need for peace among nations or factions; indeed, few analyses and indices of the Koran list *peace*.

However, it *is* mentioned. One chapter (Booty, Ch. 8: 61) states: 'If they (the enemy) should incline to peace, then incline to it too, and rely on Allah.' But another chapter (The Cow, Ch. 2: 194) urges retribution for transgressors: 'Attack anyone who attacks you to the same extent as he attacked you.'

Charis Waddy,[26] an Australian scholar (the first woman to study Arabic at Oxford) says that to the Muslim peace-making is an honourable art and one for which the Prophet himself was noted. 'He waged war when he felt driven to it by his enemies; he also reconciled the warring tribes of Arabia.' She illustrates this by referring to Muhammad's actions when he entered Mecca in 630 as a conqueror – having left it in 622 as a fugitive. 'The Meccan nobles were brought before him as prisoners, after all the bitterness and persecution they had inflicted on him – and he set them free.'

In Muslim daily life the word 'peace' is uttered very frequently – five times a day at least, or every time a Muslim prays. 'Peace be unto you,' is a traditional and conventional greeting.

An interesting exchange of letters on the subject of peace took place following the Arab-Israeli hostilities of October 1973. Mrs Ophira Telem of Acre wrote to Mrs Jehane Sadat, wife of the Egyptian president, to ask for her help in recovering the body of her brother, an Israeli frogman who was killed in a commando operation off Port Said. She described the grief of her mother and father and the sympathy extended to them by many Arab friends.

Mrs Sadat's reply expressed her condolences to the Israeli family. Her own family, she said, mourned a similar loss because the President's brother, a pilot, had been killed. Mrs Sadat wrote, 'I paid much attention to your request . . . but discovered that our forces did not find your brother's body because the ocean waves carried him far out . . . Your mother's feelings touch my heart because I too am a mother . . . I beg God that He will make up the loss your mother has suffered by a future in which she will live in peace . . . I want to emphasise to you and anyone who reads this letter that we are sincere in every step we take towards a real, just and lasting peace . . . Such grief as yours is the result of war, which we try in every way to prevent, to open the doors to peace so that no one will have to face the horrors caused by the loss of young men on both sides.'

A few years later Israel and Egypt signed a peace treaty but it remains the only real peace between any two belligerents in the Middle East.

See ISLAM: WAR: MARTYRDOM

PILGRIMAGE

For Muslims, the pilgrimage – *hajj* or *hadjdj* – to Mecca in the sacred month is one of the greatest obligations and privileges of being a member of Islam. Every Muslim is expected to make the *hajj* at least once. The journey can be long, arduous and expensive; some Muslims living in far places save all their lives for the trip, which takes place in the month of *Thil-Hijjah*, the twelfth lunar month of the Islamic calendar.

At least 2,000,000 Muslims travel to Saudi Arabia annually and most live in tents on the arid plains of Arafat, near Mecca, and perform the exhausting and complex week-long ritual of feast and prayer. Divested of all their regular clothes and ornaments, they dress in two white sheets. There is no distinction between rich and poor, black or white, Arab or non-Arab, male or female. All are equal, all must abstain from sexual intercourse. They offer their animal sacrifices and much blood is shed by throat-cutting. Hundreds of thousands of sacrificial sheep and goats are kept ready by the Bedouins and merchants, and prices are high. Only people of high rank slaughter camels. It is considered meritorious to give the flesh of the slain animals to the poor.

See MECCA: ISLAM: MUHAMMAD

PRAYER

The first chapter of the Koran forms the usual Muslim prayer and it is commonly called *Surat al-du'a'*. There are many prayers for different occasions. The Koran states: 'Prayer is a duty incumbent on the faithful, to be conducted at the appointed hours.' (4:103) It is the second of the five pillars of faith. The prayer hours are not specified in the Koran but in practice they are recognised as occurring five times a day: at dawn, midday, afternoon, evening and night. The exact times vary from country to country, even from town to town. In many countries the newspapers print daily charts showing prayer times in the major cities. Tradition says that the five-a-day schedule is a compromise between the twice-daily prayer suggested in an earlier chapter of the Koran and the 40 times a day which God demanded of Muhammad. While only five are obligatory Muslims are urged to pray at all times and on any occasion.

The believer may say his prayers wherever he is, alone or

in a group, provided he faces Mecca. Congregational prayer in a mosque is required only on Fridays at midday; group prayer is considered more meritorious than individual devotion. In some countries, notably Saudi Arabia, offices and shops close during prayer time. The urge to pray can provide situations which may surprise the Western visitor. For instance, a guard on duty at a bank may drop on his knees at the appointed hour, thus leaving the bank unprotected. The place of prayer should be clean and a worshipper may use a piece of cardboard on which to kneel and place his hands. Many Muslims use small prayer rugs. The believer knows when the hour of prayer is at hand because the call to prayer is sounded from the minaret on every mosque; the call is chanted in Arabic by a *muezzin* – but almost certainly his voice has been taped and the machine is being played from inside the mosque. The opening phrase of the chant is '*Allahu Akbar*' – God is great – and this is the dominant cultural theme of Islam. The call always includes the *shahahda*: 'God is great, God is great. I testify that there is no god but God. I testify that Muhammad brought God's message. Come to prayer, come to prayer. Come to prosperity, come to prosperity . . .'

The worshipper offers *rakatin* or 'bendings'; each part of the prayer ritual is marked by a change of position from standing, then to bending to put hands on knees, kneeling with palms on thighs, kneeling with forehead on the floor. Each *rakah* demands a certain number of prescribed acts or words, which make up a unit of prayer. Women rarely pray among men. They are probably glad of this because the prostrating part of the ritual – with the posterior elevated – would be embarrassing for them. In some places they worship in a specially set-aside area of the mosque and in others they are excluded from public prayer by tradition or law, and perform their devotions at home. It is believed, at least by men, that if women prayed with the men they would distract them.

The Koran requires that the worshipper be clean in body as well as soul. Ablution is prescribed, usually a symbolic sprinkling of water, but a full washing after sexual intercourse. Most mosques have fountains or taps where worshippers may clean their hands and feet according to ritual – and with the left hand, as it is the 'unclean' one. See KORAN: ISLAM: MUHHMAD

PRESS

In most Middle East countries the press is either government-directed or heavily censored. In recent years this has especially applied to Iran where many newspapers and journals have been closed down as 'subversive'. Editors and journalists with independent minds run the risk of being deprived of their livelihood and even of their life. In Lebanon and Iran several journalists have been murdered; a few have been found with their tongue and right hand cut off, the punishment for allegedly lying against Islam.

The standard of journalism is high in the great dailies but, given the many restrictions, it can only be routine. Investigative journalism is almost unknown. The best known English-language newspaper of the Middle East is the daily *Jerusalem Post* whose standard of journalism is the equal of any newspaper in the Western world. Hard-hitting editorially, the *Post* regards no subject as taboo and has criticised the government, the religious heirarchy, the army and, at times, every other institution. *The Middle East Times*, a weekly published in Cyprus, is another newspaper of high standard and even broader coverage of Middle East affairs than the *Jerusalem Post*.

The press is most under restraint in Algeria, Libya, Syria, Iraq, Iran, Saudi Arabia and, since 1983, in Sudan. Three good English-language weeklies are published in Qatar, others in Kuwait, and one in Egypt. French-language papers are published in Tunisia, Algeria and, in peaceful times, in Lebanon.

PROMISES

Middle Eastern people make promises rather dramatically and eloquently and they mean what they say at the moment they say it. It has to be stated, however, that promises are often not kept. There is nothing malicious about this; it is simply a fact of life. A promise made to an unbeliever has no validity nor is there any necessity to honour a truce; the purpose of a truce is to gain time and build up strength. Promises can seem tremendously impressive, since they are often made 'on honour of my mother' or 'on the memories of my ancestors'. The businessman who is promised that certain papers or information will follow him on his departure can be reasonably sure that nothing will arrive. The only way to ensure that a promise is fulfilled is to keep asking, especially in person. Importunate letters are rarely answered.

QATAR

The tiny (10,360 sq. km.) country of Qatar is ruled by an Emir, Sheikh Kalifa bin Hamad al-Thani, who, like all indigenous Qataris, is of the strict Wahabi sect of Islam. Only 60,000 of the population of 200,000 hold Qatar citizenship while 40,000 are Iranians, 25,000 Palestinians and another 25,000 Pakistanis. Women have slightly higher status in Qatar than in other Arab countries, but there are none in public life.

Despite the ethnic medley, Qatar has enjoyed a high degree of internal stability since 1970. Its extensive social services, enlightened attitude towards the Press and the

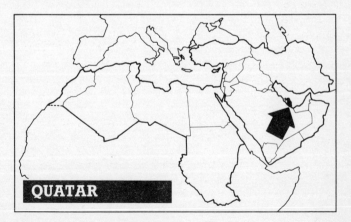

QUATAR

close links enjoyed by the emir and his cabinet with the Palestinian community has helped create a peaceful atmosphere. Many of the Palestinians hold senior administrative and professional posts in the government. Shi'a dissent appears to be less in Qatar than in other Gulf states. Qatar favours a policy of non-intervention in the area, both by the USA and the Soviet Union.

Qatar's earnings from its deposits abroad – that is, money made from oil and then invested in foreign countries – amount to 200 million dollars a year. By the mid-1980s the country is likely to be earning as much from 'capital exports' as from oil itself. Because Qatar has huge reserves of gas – probably larger than Holland's great Groningen field – it can look forward to a financially secure future even after the oil runs out. For defence it relies on its stronger neighbours, such as Saudi Arabia, and on its membership of the Gulf Co-operation Council. Sheikh Khalifa's policy of 'not getting involved' is probably Qatar's best protection.

RACISM

A good deal of study needs to be done on racism in the Middle East but it certainly exists among Arab peoples and in Iran. This is only natural because of the direct Koranic statement that the Arab Islamic people are the best ever created and the most favoured by God. Even within Islam racism exists, so that the Iranian Shi'as consider themselves superior to the Sunnis and the pure Arabs consider themselves superior to the Kurds. The Saudis, since they come from the region where Muhammad received the Koran, tend to regard themselves as the 'best of Islam', while the Syrians, with an ancient recorded history, look down upon those with a shorter history.

Upper and middle class Egyptians have a pronounced sense of race while the Turks, conscious of having been the greatest imperialists in the Middle East, see the Arab peoples as inferior. All the Arabic peoples consider themselves superior to the Israelis because the Jews are by Koranic decree inferior to Muslims.

Muslims also see Christians as inferior and this racist

attitude was the root cause of the Sudanese Civil War, 1960 – 77; the Arabs of the north wished to impose their authority on the Christians of the south. This issue again became critical in 1983 when Muslims demanded that the Christians should be considered *dhimmi* or second-class citizens, in accordance with the Koran. President Nimieri's government decided to 'Islamise' the south.

Racism is also evident in Mauretania where the Muslim-Arab Berbers and Moors keep at least 100,000 negro slaves. The treatment of Kurds and neglect of their human rights by Iranians, Iraqis and Syrians has a strong racist basis. The Armenians, Circassians and above all, the Copts, complain that they are victims of racism.

See ARABS: KORAN: ISLAM: JUDAISM

RAMADAN

Ramadan is the only month mentioned by name in the Koran – as the month in which the Holy Book was 'sent down'. For Muslims it is a time of intensified devotion and mutual forgiveness; in practice it is a rigorous discipline and ordeal which has no parallel in Christian and Jewish experience. For 28 days there is an absolute prohibition of all bodily sustenance by whatever means during daylight hours – in some Islamic countries it is an offence to swallow your own spittle – and an abstinence from sexual activity. The ban on drinking imposes great hardship when Ramadan occurs in summer – the Muslim year follows the lunar calendar so Ramadan 'moves'. Trade and industry are largely at a standstill, especially in the hot season.

People are inclined to make up during the night for the deprivations of the day. As sleeping is not forbidden during the fast they often sleep a part of the day; the night is given up to all sorts of pleasures and many people gorge themselves as a way of balancing their daily starvation. Towards evening smokers listen with rapt attention to the radio so that when the end of the day's abstinence is officially announced, often by a cannon shot, they can light up at once. Muslims are not pleasant people to know during Ramadan and they are the first to admit it; they become

tense, irritable, unco-operative, impatient and, as drivers, dangerous. Western businessmen in particular should try to avoid visiting Muslim countries during Ramadan, because little can be done.
See BUSINESS

REFUGEES

Waves of refugees are part of the history of the Middle East from Roman times. In this century the Armenians, Nestorians (or Assyrians), Circassians, Turkish and Greek Cypriots, Christian Sudanese, Somalis, Eritreans, Palestinians, Jews and Christian Lebanese have all become refugees. The most publicised refugees are the Palestinians; about 600,000 fled from the new state of Israel at the time of partition in 1948. The advice to leave their homes came from their own leaders and the leaders of the Arab nations who declared war against Israel rather than from any direct threat from the new Israeli state; they expected to win the war and to be able to return.

The 600,000 Palestinian refugees of 1948 scattered throughout the Middle East, the majority settling in refugee camps administered by the UN Relief and Works Agency (UNRWA). Only Jordan has granted its Palestinian residents citizenship and of the $2 billion contributed internationally by the UN member nations to finance UNRWA's work less than 5 per cent has come from the 21 Arab states. During the war of June 1967 – the Six-Day War – other Palestinians from the West Bank of the Jordan became refugees.

The Gulf states readily absorbed their Palestinians but the major Arab countries used them as political pawns. Nasser's Egypt was particularly culpable in this respect, for Nasser believed that the Arab world could be unified around the plight of the Palestinians. As fast as UNRWA erected good homes for the Palestinians in Lebanon, Nasser's agents destroyed them. In this way the Palestinians were forced to live in camps, which become hotbeds of discontent. Oppression by the PLO in southern Lebanon later forced the Christians of many villages to leave their homes.

Simultaneously with the first flight of Palestinians in 1948, another great refugee movement was in progress, that of the Jews from Arab lands where they had lived for millenia. Between 1948 and 1957 more than 850,000 Jews were driven out of their homelands, leaving behind an inestimable fortune in property. During the worst pogroms, 260,000 Jews left Morocco, 14,000 Algeria, 35,000 Libya, 30,000 Egypt, 130,000 Iraq, 50,500 Yemen, 4,500 Syria, 6,000 Lebanon and 56,000 Tunisia. Made homeless virtually overnight, most of these Jews turned to Israel as their refuge. In effect, Israel was built on refugees, first of all from Nazi Europe, then from the hopelessness of ruined postwar Europe (those who were lucky enough to survive the Holocaust) and finally from the Arab world.

See JEWS: PALESTINE LIBERATION ORGANISATION: WEST BANK

SADAT, President Anwar

Sadat was relatively unknown outside Egypt when he succeeded Nasser as president of Egypt and therefore as political leader of the Arab world. Nasser's reputation had been so great that initially the quieter, more pragmatic Sadat was underestimated both in his own country and abroad. At first he continued Nasser's policy of hostility towards Israel and pursued a war of attrition along the Suez Canal. In October 1973 he personally planned and launched 'the Great Crossing' – an all-out war against Israel. The Egyptian forces were successful in the beginning but the Israelis counter-crossed the canal and surrounded an entire Egyptian army. Under international pressure the war ended inconclusively though Egypt regained part of Sinai. The event made Sadat a hero in the Arab world.

As military spending was bankrupting Egypt, Sadat sought peace with Israel in what became known as 'the Sadat initiative'. He flew to Israel and was received by the Israeli parliament. As a result a peace treaty was signed on March 26, 1980 and by 1981 Israel had returned the entire Sinai to Egypt. The peace was opposed by the Arab world and many factions threatened to assassinate Sadat. He met his death during an army parade at the hands of some of his own soldiers, who had been incited by Islamic extremists. Sadat's peace with Israel was one of the most courageous and most dramatic achievements of the century in the Middle East.

Gaddafi sent his congratulations to Sadat's assassins and declared Sunday a holiday to celebrate the murder, 'in response to the euphoria which has swept the Arab nations with the disappearance of the Egyptian President.' After the funeral Libyan government radio announced, 'Sadat lived like a Jew and he died like a Jew.' Syria joined other radical nations in abusing the dead Sadat. The assassination was termed as 'execution' and the Ba'ath party newspaper, *Tishrin* warned, 'By continuing the path of Sadat, by continuing efforts to make Egypt an agent and a satellite of US imperialism, his heirs face the same fate as the traitor.'

The General Confederation of the Iraqi Trade Unions, 'greeted the Arab people in proud Egypt and the Egyptian Army who bravely and boldly exacted the just punishment that was decided by the Arab people's conference in Baghdad against the renegade traitor.' In South Yemen Aden Domestic Service announced that the assassination was 'the end of a tyrannical traitor who sold himself to the Zionist and American circles and imposed himself as a tyrannical ruler on the struggling Egyptian people. Sadat's violent death is also regarded as a lesson to those who want to join the road of treason and surrender to imperialism . . .'

SAUDI ARABIA

The Arab world revolves around Saudi Arabia because of its wealth from oil, its historical status in relation to Islam, the influence of its royal family of 5,000 princes and its central geographical position. Regarded as a moderate Arab state, Saudi Arabia considers itself the custodian of the Islamic legacy and this gives its leaders great political influence throughout the 44 countries of the Islamic world.

Yet the country came into being as a nation only in 1932 when Abdul Aziz of the Wahabi family set himself up as

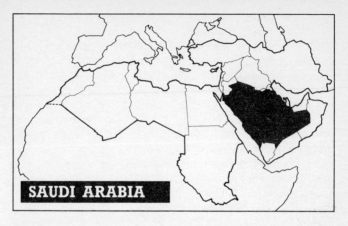

SAUDI ARABIA

absolute monarch and based the new state's political and
legal systems on the Koran and *Hadith*; there is no written
constitution. Religious institutions operate side by side with
political institutions to ensure that the orthodoxy of the
ruling Wahabis is supreme. A body of senior 'clerics'
(*ulema*) controls religious life and enforcement is left to the
much-feared *Mutawwah* or religious police. They impose
punishments which are sometimes harsh, arbitrary and
swift; for instance, shopkeepers slow to close at prayer times
are caned, as are women who show too much ankle beneath
their black gowns.

Aziz was succeeded by King Saud whose extravagance
and his attempted plot to assassinate President Nasser
brought the country to a crisis. Faisal, the Crown Prince,
was given effective power as prime minister in 1958 and
held power until he was assassinated in 1975. He was
succeeded by King Khalid. Nepotism is the norm in Saudi
Arabia and several senior members of the royal family hold
influential positions in the Government and in the State.

While the population is largely of the Sunni sect, Saudi
Arabia has 250,000 Shi'a nationals in the eastern province,
which is only just across the Gulf from Iran. It is through
this minority that the Iranian revolutionaries are trying to
bring about a revolution in Saudi Arabia. As one of many
ways of protecting itself, the royal family has employed

units of the Pakistani army as palace guards and protectors of some of the holy places.

The per capita income of the population of 9·5 million is high but many Saudis have three part-time full-paid jobs. A man may own a shop or stall in a bazaar, hold down a job in a government department for a few hours a day, and operate as a taxi-driver in the evening. Many of life's necessities are subsidised by the government and thus kept at artificially low prices.

The world's largest oil producer, Saudi Arabia is immensely wealthy and officially-held foreign assets are about $140 billion. These overseas assets generate interest at the rate of $10 billion a year. Saudi Arabia is visited by about 3 million pilgrims a year, earning foreign exchange from other Muslim countries. Heavy invisible outgoings include payments for services and remittances of the 2 million foreigners working in Saudi Arabia. The government would prefer not to have these foreign residents but rapid and massive industrialisation is the key to Saudi development.

The kingdom is one of the largest aid donors. As the second largest lender to the International Monetary Fund, Saudi Arabia in 1978 took a seat on the Executive Board of Governors, a position permanently guaranteed. Its quota in the fund is $2·1 billion and its voting strength is 3·5 per cent.

The Saudi rulers labour at keeping the Arabs as united as possible – though they refuse to co-operate with Libya; they hate Gaddafi as much as he hates them. They work through money rather than through appeals for Islamic or Arab brotherhood. They finance the PLO, the Syrians and the Syrian's enemies, the Iraqis. During the Gulf War the Saudis gave Iraq $25,000 million.

Saudi Arabia has armed forces totalling 51,000 and a national guard of 25,000 equipped with the best and latest equipment that money can buy, including thousands of missiles and some US-supplied AWAC early-warning command aircraft.

Despite its international importance and its generally pro-Western stance, Saudi Arabia is socially backward.

Women have few rights and the education of girls is not considered as important as that of boys; females are strictly guarded and those who bring shame to their family – by a clandestine relationship with a man, for instance – are severely punished. Foreign women living in the country or visiting it as tourists must observe all the regulations governing female conduct; for example, no woman may drive a car.

Some Saudi girls study abroad where they live and dress as Westerners. It is interesting to see these girls met by their family at the international airport when they return home. While the men and children surround the homecomer her mother and perhaps an aunt hastily cover up her Western attire by throwing over her the traditional shapeless black gown. They do this for fear she will bring shame to the family – and the real risk of being reprimanded by the religious police.

The country can be exasperatingly difficult for foreigners to understand and it is certainly an expensive country for them to visit. It is also a dull one since there are no legitimate diversions. Western people not infrequently find themselves in prison because of offences against the alcohol laws. There are other dangers too, especially for single girls; some have been murdered and others have disappeared. Western people involved in any kind of dispute with Saudi nationals can expect no official help; the visitor is always in the wrong.

Despite much publicity about non-Muslims being banned from Mecca some visitors still head for it across the desert road – in summer so hot that tyres explode – until they come to blue and white signs, in English, a few miles from Mecca. They warn the non-Muslim traveller to turn off the road; he must make a circuitous detour around the city and armed guards make sure that no stranger reaches it.

See MECCA: LAW: WOMEN: ISLAM: FAHD, King

SEX

See LOVE AND SEX

SHI'A ISLAM

The word *shi'a* means partisan and Shi'a Muslims are those who reject the first three caliphs who succeeded Muhammad. They are partisans or followers of Ali, Muhammad's cousin and son-in-law, who, they say, was designated by Muhammad as his successor. He was endowed by divine will, the Shi'a world claims, with spiritual as well as temporal authority. The correct line of succession, they say, was through the descendants of Ali and the prophet's daughter Fatima. Ali had as good a claim to the caliphate as anyone but was passed over three times, finally to be chosen on the death of Uthman in 655. Outmanoeuvred by his enemies, he was assassinated in 661.

Shi'as believe that it was Ali who compiled the Koran and codified Arabic grammar. He was not the fourth in a line of caliphs, but the first in a line of divinely guided imams. The imamate is a fundamental precept of Shi'ism and the one that most distinguishes it from Sunnism. Shi'ism rejects the Sunni belief that the divine law bestows upon the people themselves the authority to select the ruler of an Islamic society. This is why Shi'as feel compelled to overthrow Sunni regimes and set divinely guided clerics in their place.

In Sunni societies all believers are said to be equal before God, but Shi'as have a kind of clergy whose members have an elevated spiritual status, with Khomeini as their head. Even before the Iranian revolution the network of ayatollahs and mullahs in Iran not only conducted the country's religious affairs but also controlled great wealth, owned estates and developed a nation-wide political organisation with independent finance. It has no parallel in Sunni countries.

About 15 per cent of all Muslims are Shi'as; they form the greater part of the population of Iran, where Shi'ism is the official religion, and they make a major part of the population of Lebanon, about half the Iraqis and a sixth of Pakistanis. There are an estimated 250,000 Shi'as in Saudi Arabia.

Other distinctions between Shi'ism and Sunnism are more profound than a dispute over succession. Shi'ism has unique characteristics that affect the political as well as the religious behaviour of its adherents. The violent deaths of Ali and his son Hussein instilled in the Shi'as an admiration and even a desire for martyrdom – and they are still prepared to demonstrate this. Shi'a Muslims are passionately devoted not only to martyrdom but to belief in saints, to worshipping of holy men at their tombs and to a mystical faith in the eventual return of the vanished Imam, a spiritual leader designated by God to guide them. Because of all this Shi'as are demonstrative and they indulge in physical exhibitions of spiritual devotion that sets them apart from Sunnis. Shi'as argue that their interpretation is a natural development of what was always inherent in the Koran.

For Western policy-makers, the most important distinction between Sunnism and Shi'ism is not a religious but a political one. Shi'ism is a revolutionary, anti-Western culturally uniform force, which gives it a broad appeal that can cut across the borders of state and language. Iraq confronted this force while the weak states of the Gulf compromised with it. The Shi'as of Khomeini claim to be closer to the precepts of the Koran than the Sunnis are. The West misunderstands Shi'ism at its peril.

See ISLAM: MARTYRDOM: PARADISE: ASSASSINS

SLAVERY

Ownership of human beings and their exploitation continues in parts of the Middle East as it has done for centuries. It is the area in which the largest number of slaves still exist and are traded. In Algeria, Mauretania and Morocco slaves are used to a large extent as household servants and they are usually the children of slaves; they stay with the same 'owning' family for generations.

Libya is one of the few countries to suffer from the problem of under-population. It appears that a large number of black slaves are imported to alleviate this manpower shortage but it is unlikely that the Libyan government actually imports these slaves. In Egypt, where slavery is illegal and has been outlawed, the country's form of land ownership and the indebtedness it gives rise to among the fellaheen creates a situation similar to serfdom; the fellaheen are tied to the land for generation after generation through their debts.

The greatest number of slaves live on the Arabian peninsula itself. Jonathan Derrick[27] in his book *Africa's Slaves Today* says:

> There are few parts of the world where slavery has lasted so persistently as in . . . Saudi Arabia, Yemen, Oman . . . Africa here still presents what geography destined it to be for in previous centuries – a source of slaves for kings, sheikhs, merchants and other property owners in Arabia.

The largest number of them is to be found in Saudi Arabia itself. In 1962 when King Faisal deposed his brother, Ibn Saud, he proclaimed slave trading and slavery illegal. There is a great gap, however, between the proclamation and its implementation. During the Holy Month of Ramadan each year hundreds of thousands of black Muslim pilgrims make their way to the holy cities of Mecca and Medina. This holy pilgrimage always turns out to be more expensive than is anticipated because of the expensive fees which the pilgrim is charged. The pilgrim's only solution is to sell his servants and sometimes his children. It is believed that up to 20,000 black Africans, together with some Pakistanis, Bangladeshis and Indonesians remain in Saudi Arabia each year under this practice.

South Yemen has abolished slavery but in North Yemen ownership and trading in slaves has not been declared illegal and has not stopped. Oman, Dubai, Qatar and most of the Gulf sheikdoms trade in slaves. Slavery also exists in Iran and has had a resurgence under Khomeini.

Islam does not forbid the ownership of slaves but lays down stringent regulations to ensure their good treatment; the implementation of these regulations differs from family to family and tribe to tribe.

Many European girls who get positions as nannies or 'companions' to Middle East families living in the West, find, when they accompany the families back to the Middle East, that they are little more than slaves. Unable to leave certain countries without an exit visa they are friendless and alone. Girls who have found themselves in this predicament have even had difficulty in getting money due to them. Much publicity has been given to certain cases.

See KORAN: MECCA: PILGRIMAGE: SAUDI ARABIA

SOCIETY

Traditional Arab Muslim society is far from egalitarian. The Koran itself refers to the divine creation of class differences. One verse (ch. 6, verse 165) says that 'God hath raised some of you above others by various grades . . .' and another (ch. 4, verse 36) urges the believer: 'Covet not the gifts by which God hath raised some of you above others. The men shall have a portion according to their deserts, and the women a portion according to their deserts.'

Middle East society starts with the family, is patterned on it, and extends outwards from it. Born into a group, the individual remains a part of it through no special effort to please or belong. If he fails in his role within his family he might be regarded as a bad character but he does not lose his membership. Wider contacts come through the family and its extensions. Friends are chosen among relatives, family friends and their children. Hamady[4] says that 'Arabs are born into a group and many never join another group, except under foreign influences in the city.' Hamady also makes the point that even political parties are not formed mainly on the basis of political or social issues but on the basis of familial, religious and social factions.

Social classes are based on occupation, income and power and never on education, family or other criteria common in the West because these are merely steps *towards* occupation, income and power. A peasant accepts the fact that he is socially inferior to a landlord, merchant or government clerk; he may resent his social class and may try to rise to a higher one but he is not likely to deny the fact of his low status. Morroe Berger,[11] director of Middle Eastern Studies at Princeton University, suggests the following classification in Middle East Arab society:

- Big landowners, bankers, industrialists and highest government and military leaders.

- Higher civil servants and army officers, independent professionals (doctors, lawyers, engineers) higher intellectuals, religious leaders

- Lower professions (teachers, journalists, pharmacists, white-collar workers in government and private enterprise)

- Shopkeepers, skilled workers, artisans, soldiers with technical qualifications

- Peasants, labourers, service workers, the army rank and file.

- Slaves – where they still exist.

This classification is based on Western concepts and it does not follow that the values and attitudes and powers of the classes so called are identical with the West. The most important differences are in the relative size of each class and the degree of influence each exerts on society. The agricultural class is far more numerous, proportionally, than in the West, and it is weaker politically. It is also a landless class living at bare subsistence level. The working class is also weak but not numerous (as in the West) because modern industry employs only a small proportion of the labour force. The peasants and urban workers are still so poor and depressed that, except for a very small section of the latter which has recently begun to find articulate leaders, they remain outside the political community.

The social classes which formerly controlled affairs have lost much of their power with the advent of military regimes which owe no allegiance to older classes. The importance of social classes in the Middle East lies not in Western interpretations of the classes but in the way the Arabs themselves conceive class.

The pecking order is clear and emphatic and people of any class will speak brusquely and deal firmly, even harshly, with people in a lower class. This is nowhere more evident than in the armies. Officers are rarely seen with their men and it is never considered their duty to train the rank and file; this is the function of the NCOs. Officers turn up only for ceremonial occasions. It is noticeable in war that the majority of officers consider themselves too important to be risked.

See CHILDREN: CRIME: FAMILY: HONOUR: WOMEN: LOVE AND SEX

SOVIET UNION IN THE MIDDLE EAST

In centuries past the Russians were drawn towards the Mediterranean and the Indian Ocean in their ambition to have warm-water ports, even more than the possibility of acquiring territory and wealth. This has always explained their attacks on Turkey, as the gateway to the Mediterranean, and on Afghanistan and the northwest provinces of India as the path to the Indian Ocean and Persian Gulf.

In recent times the Soviet leaders have seen control of the oilfields of the Middle East and of the international water-ways – the Persian Gulf, Straits of Hormuz, Red Sea, Straits of Bab el-Mandeb and the Suez Canal – as vital in any major war against the West. Western interests in the Middle East were in themselves enough to attract the Soviet Union to the area, since these influences had to be countered. To this end, Soviet leaders have wooed the Arab states with offers of money, arms, technology and friendship. Without excep-tion, the Arab states, Iran and Turkey have become diplo-matic 'targets', though priorities change according to stra-tegic circumstance. In 1956 the Soviet Union threatened to intervene in the Suez War, in 1957 it sent representatives to the Afro-Asian Conference in Cairo and also exerted much influence in Syria and Iraq. Nasser was invited to Moscow in 1958 and from then on many Arab leaders accepted similar invitations. The Soviet recognised Kuwait in 1963 and Jordan in 1964 and President Kruschev attended the opening of the Aswan dam the same year.

In 1964, with the foundation of the PLO, the Russians discovered that the way to make friends of all Arabs was to support the Arab nations and the PLO against Israel. This policy made their diplomats welcome in most Arab capitals, particularly Cairo, Damascus, Amman and Baghdad. In

1966 the USA ceased to give aid to Egypt, which fell into the arms of the Soviet Union; a tremendous amount of Russian military material reached Egypt before the Six-Day War of June 1967 – and much of it was captured by the victorious Israelis. By the end of 1970 the Soviet had stationed 200 pilots and about 15,000 men in missile crews in Egypt and were manning 80 missile sites.

At this time the Soviet was supplying vast quantities of arms and equipment to Syria, Libya, Iraq, Algeria and to the PLO at its bases in Lebanon, Syria and Jordan. In 1971, with unexpected boldness, Sadat expelled all Russian advisers and specialists from Egypt, leaving Moscow to look to Damascus and Baghdad for a new centre of influence in the Middle East. Nearly all equipment that the Syrian army used in the 1973 war against Israel came from the Soviet bloc countries.

In 1982, when Israel attacked the PLO in Lebanon, the Soviet did not respond to their pleas for help and was discredited in the Arab world. This led, in 1983 – 4, to a carefully planned campaign to re-establish Russian influence. The Soviet built up Syria as the strongest Arab nation, with the latest missiles, including SS-21s. The Russians encouraged Syria in its policy of 'Greater Syria' – that is, incorporation of Lebanon into Syria – of refusing to withdraw from Lebanon and of belligerence towards both the USA and Israel. At the same time, the Russians provided Iraq with much *material* to replace that lost in the war against Iran. Until 1983 Iraq regarded the USA as its friend; the Soviet offer to double what the Americans offered changed all that. In 1985 the USA regained lost ground.

Soviet policy in the Middle East is simple and direct – to destabilise the region by preventing the USA and other Western nations from bringing about an Arab-Israeli peace or any other form of peace. Another objective is to disrupt the free flow of oil from the Middle East to the West and to Japan. During 1983 – 5 the Russians were sending a stream of official and 'unofficial' delegations to all Arab countries in an attempt to undercut American – and therefore Western – influence. After English, Arabic is considered the most important language for Russian officials, because of expanding Soviet interests in the Arab world.

See individual Arab countries: IRAN: TURKEY: UNITED STATES IN THE MIDDLE EAST

SUDAN

With an area of 2,505,813 sq. km. Sudan is Africa's largest country and it has some of the continent's biggest problems. The word Sudan derives from the Arabic '*Bilad al-Sudan*' – the Land of the Blacks – and it was applied by Islamic nomads. While its population of 20 million is predominantly Sunni Muslim it has millions of Christians in the south. About $3\frac{1}{2}$ times the size of Texas, the country stretches more than 1,000 miles from the barren deserts of the north to the mountains and rain forests of the south. It borders eight other States. More than 1,000 languages and dialects are spoken by as many ethnic groups, and cultural, linguistic and religious diversity makes it difficult for Sudanese to behave in a unified way. Demands for secession in the south recurrently simmer.

The President, Field Marshal Gaafar Muhammad Nimieri, is also Prime Minister, Minister of Defence, Commander-in-Chief of the armed forces and president of the official news agency. Naturally, he leads the only

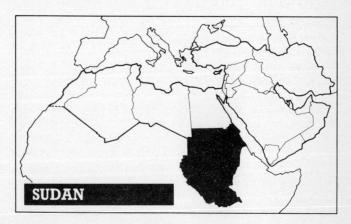

permitted political party, the Sudanese Socialist Union. There is a National People's Assembly of 250 members, and 125 are elected by universal suffrage, but no deputy sits without Nimieri's personal approval.

Nimieri came to power in a bloodless coup on May 25, 1969. His movement was stated to be 'democratic, socialist and non-aligned' and it was inspired by Nasser's Free Officers Movement in Egypt. His rule has seen great bloodshed. The armed Ansar sect of Islam were decisively defeated by the army in 1970 and at least 27,000 (possibly as many as 30,000) were massacred on Aba Island in the Nile. Their leader, Sadiq el-Mahdi, the great grandson of Muhammad Ahmed, who had caused the British so much trouble in colonial days, was sent into exile and lived in England.

Nimieri has worked hard to reconcile differences since the end of Sudan's 17-year civil war in 1977, in which half a million people died. An Islamic revival in the north forces him into Muslim dominion even more. His handling of the country's collapsing economy and his plans to divide the south into three smaller regions are resented by southerners. They see it as a tactic to weaken political opposition. One of Nimieri's biggest failings has been his neglect in developing road, river and air transport between the two regions. Communications are unreliable. Sudan is one of the world's most refugee-jammed nations; many of these refugees, from famine and fighting, come from neighbouring Ethiopia.

Most of Sudan's economic problems stem from the high price of Arab oil; the Arab oil producers have made no concession to Sudan in its financial plight. Arabic, the official language, is gradually asserting itself and pushing out English as the *lingua franca*. This too has aroused bitterness among the southern educated elite. So has the government policy of building new mosques and its plans to introduce the Shari'a or Islamic law south of the 'Arab belt'. In the Arab north the harsh Shari'a punishments are as strictly imposed as in Saudi Arabia. An open air stadium has been built at Kober, near Khartoum, for the public display of Islamic punishments, such as stoning to death for women adulterers, flogging for certain offences including drinking of alcohol, and hand amputation for thieves.

Such is the geopolitical importance of Sudan that Nimieri has established himself a reputation as a stabiliser between the two worlds of Africa and the Middle East. But he is walking a political tight-rope in his attempts to reconcile the extremist Muslim Brotherhood and the opposition group, the Mahdist Movement, led by Sadiq el-Mahdi, now back in Sudan and in prison. Libyan subversion remains a major concern in Sudan. Nimieri sees the hand of Libya – and of Moscow – everywhere. There is constant fear that Libyans might step up their backing of some Islamic opposition.

Because of hostility from the National Front – a mixture of the Muslim Brotherhood and the other fundamentalist Islamic groups, Ansar and Khatmia – Sudan can expect much conflict and violence. Nimieri has come to the conclusion that it is safer to alienate the Christians of the south than the Islamic extremists of the north. In 1983 Sudan veered markedly towards Islamic fundamentalism, which means strict application of the Shari'a Islamic law and its punishments for wrongdoers. Sudan is bankrupt and the Arab states which keep it going, notably Saudi Arabia, have told Nimieri that their price for economic help is that he make Sudan a wholly Islamic state.

The country is too important, economically and strategically, to be ignored either by the Arabs who require food and military security, or by the USA whose foreign policy relies heavily on 'go-between' nations in its opposition to communism. This explains why so much economic aid has been forthcoming from the USA – $250 million a year – and from the rich Arab countries.*

See KORAN: FANATICISM: LAW

* President Nimieri was deposed in a bloodless coup on 6 April 1985. The new military ruler, General Abdul-Rahman Swaredehab, promised to return the nation to civilian democratic government.

SUNNI MUSLIMS

The Sunnis are the Muslims who stress their adherence to the path (sunna) of the Prophet and are known as the orthodox group, though a better term would be the standard group. They constitute 85 per cent of the Islamic community. In only one country of the Arab world, Iraq, are the Sunnis in a minority, but the Sunnis hold the major positions in the government and the economy. Sunni Muslims generally regard the Shi'as as deviants from Islam and they often quote the *hadith* (traditional saying of Muhammad), 'He who tires of my sunna does not belong to me' meaning that the Shi'as are *not* following the right path.

Historically, the Sunni Muslims accepted the worldly authority of the Caliphs who succeeded Muhammad. The Caliphate came into being to provide a successor who had adequate rank and dignity. The Caliphs had no spiritual role in the way that Muhammad had, but they were master administrators. The first was Abu Bakr, then 'Umar, both fathers-in-law of Muhammad. Three of the first four Caliphs were murdered, a token of the violence which was to permeate the Islamic world. The Sunnis followed the Caliph of the time, no matter how he attained his supreme position.

In the same way over the centuries and in their various communities they came to follow a sheikh, emir, prince, king or president. From time to time 'holy men' have appeared within Sunni Islam, claiming to be the Mahdi, 'the expected one', but few of them found favour for long. One of the great quarrels Shi'a Muslims have with Sunni Islam is that Sunnis accept monarchs. To the devout Shi'a, such as an Iranian ayatollah, monarchs have no place in Islam.

Sunni Muslims are less concerned than Shi'a Muslims about points of dogma and interpretation, and they are less prone to division and discord. They do not have the profoundly passionate spirit of the Shi'as but like them they have a particularly holy day; the ninth day of the first Muslim month. This is the fast of the *Ashura* and it is observed by the devout of the entire Sunni world. It is also holy on 'historical grounds', since on that day Noah left the ark. In Mecca the door of the Islamic holiest of holies, the Ka'ba, is opened for visitors on the day of the *Ashura*. As with the corresponding Shi'a *Muharram*, foreign visitors are

advised to stay away from devout worshippers on the day of
the *Ashura*.

See SHI'A MUSLIMS: ISLAM: MUHAMMAD: KORAN: HADITH

SYRIA

In the 1980s Syria emerged as the most difficult Arab
country for the West to deal with because of its militant
stand in regard to Israel, Lebanon and the United States. As
the Middle East country most favoured by the Soviet Union
and the only one likely to go to war against Israel it has the
potential to disrupt the entire delicate fabric of the Middle
East.

More than 90 per cent of the population of 9·5 million is
Muslim, mostly Sunni, with Shi'a, Ismaili, Druze, Alawite
and Yazidi minorities. Less than 10 per cent of the
population is Christian, divided among Greek, Armenian
and Syrian Orthodox and Catholic persuasians as well as the
Maronites. About 4,000 Jews, all in Damascus, are
prevented from leaving Syria because they may be useful in
any bargaining with Israel.

Denial of human rights in Syria has long been of concern
to the international community. The repressive nature of
President Hafez al-Assad's regime and the state of
emergency which has existed during his whole term of

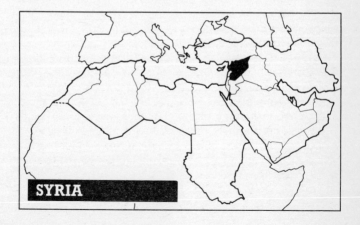

office, since 1970, makes the maintenance of civilised standards virtually impossible. Amnesty International lists six main abuses of human rights, including torture, arbitrary execution and the lack of basic legal safeguards. Amnesty believes there are 10,000 political prisoners.

The root of the problem lies in Syria's internal political structure. Assad heads a regime dominated by the Alawite sect which represents only 10 per cent of Syria's population. The Sunni majority resent the Alawite ascendancy which is maintained only because of Assad's control over the army, his ruthless suppression of all opposition and widespread denial of individual freedom. The *Observer* stated, March 27, 1981: 'As well as massive repression at home, assassination squads are apparently now being sent Gaddafi-style to liquidate troublesome exiles in Europe. To meet terror, Assad has resorted to ferocious counter-terror . . . indiscriminate arrests, beatings and torture, shoot-outs and mass killings.'

The main instruments of Assad's repression are the Special Defence units of Syria's security forces, an élite of 25,000. Until 1984 these units were controlled by Rifa'at Assad, the president's brother. In June 1980 the SDU killed 17 officers for 'criticising' Rifa'at Assad; in August 17 civilians were rounded up and killed for the same reason. Another of the President's brothers, Jamil, commands a group within the SDU responsible for defending the Alawite community. Assad's cousin, Adnan, controls a commando force operating around Damascus while two of Assad's nephews hold senior posts in the army.

Syria accuses its Arab neighbours of arming the banned Muslim Brotherhood, an Islamic fundamentalist group which opposes Assad's régime. In December 1980 200 Brotherhood supporters were shot in the public square in Aleppo and in January 1981 300 members of the movement being held in Tadmor prison, Palmyra, were buried alive. In February 1982 the Syrian army took over Hama, after a rebellion; at least 15,000 males, including boys aged 10, were executed.

Syria has been vilified in much of the Arab world for its support of Ayatollah Khomeini's regime in the Iran–Iraq

War. King Hussein of Jordan and President Hussein of Iraq have encouraged efforts to depose Assad. In 1976 Syria sent a 30,000-man army of occupation into Lebanon to support its claim that Lebanon is really part of Syria. That army numbered 40,000 in 1984. Heavily armed by the Soviet, and in effective control of half the PLO, Syria intends one day to launch a blitzkrieg on Israel that will destroy the Jewish state before its army can react as it has done in the past. The terrorist acts of 1983 against the USA, France and Israel were organised in Damascus.

Syria would be bankrupt if it did not receive financial aid from various Arab countries. Because it was the only country 'standing up to Israel' following the separate peace treaty between Egypt and Israel, the 1979 Arab summit granted Syria an annual income of 1,850 million dollars.

The army has gradually replaced government bodies in a number of spheres, in particular internal security, education, economic planning and trade. The State is militarised to a degree rare even in the Middle East. Secret servicemen are ubiquitous in the civil service, schools, universities, trade unions and political parties. The press in Syria is strictly government controlled and editors and journalists who disobey orders are dealt with severely; several were murdered or 'disappeared' in 1983.

More than 75 per cent of Syrian women are illiterate despite guarantees of equality in the 1973 Constitution. Women are not allowed to leave the country without government permission and the Moral Intelligence Department investigates the background of every woman who applies for a job in the civil service. Only 11 per cent of women work outside the home; no more than 26 per cent of secondary school pupils are girls.

Syria is an odd mixture of official and often half-hearted socialism, of heady Arabic slogans, of a shadowy world of entrepreneurs who somehow manage to get word about government tenders before they are published and inform potential clients in the West. Their fees range from 10 per cent to as high as 35 per cent. It is here that the Levantine art of 'fixing' was born, far outclassing the wily Lebanese themselves. It is estimated that since 1973 5,000 Syrian businessmen have become dollar millionaires. It is easy to cream off substantial commissions between nationalised companies and foreign firms because the state controls all major development schemes, 80 per cent of imports and 90 per cent of exports. Smuggling is rife and the biggest single smuggler is allegedly the army. Another thriving practice is bribery which has become rife in Syria since 1970. Before that, civil servants used to take the offer of even the tiniest gift as a personal insult. Nowadays liberal backhanders are essential. Luxury hotels accommodate a stream of Western contract-seekers. Nubile Syrian 'hostesses', gold chains around ankles, grace the surrounds of hotel swimming pools.

The EEC remains Syria's main trading partner but Western companies are often discouraged by restrictions in the private sector, delays in settling invoices, and massive administrative red tape. Any Westerner visiting Syria should realise that secret police may follow him throughout his stay and that his belongings may be searched and his mail read.

See ASSAD: LEBANON: PALESTINE LIBERATION ORGANISATION

TERRORISM

Middle East terrorism began with the Assassins and was common throughout the centuries. Contemporary terrorism, in a systematic and organised sense, began in the 1960s with the formation of various Palestinian and other Arab groups to strike at targets within Israel and at Israelis and Jews further afield. Some Palestinian Arab para-military and terrorist organisations had been in existence before the PLO came into being in 1964 but it soon enveloped all of them.

State-employed terrorists from Russia and Eastern European countries have always operated against their own hostile nationals abroad but the Arabs, through the PLO, were the first to 'export' terror in the form of training, weapons, explosives, finance and practical help for foreign groups. The Palestinians, too, have created the slogan

'There are no innocent people.' Some foreigners, caught up in inter-Arab feuds and Arab attacks against Israeli and Jewish targets, have been killed.

During the 1970s terrorist groups from many countries turned to the Arab organisations for assistance. Thus the PLO groups were allies, at the same time, of both extreme right and extreme left factions. George Habash's Popular Front for the Liberation of Palestine (PFLP), a far-left Marxist-Leninist group, has ties with extreme right neo-Nazi organisations. Terrorists in at least 31 countries look to the PLO as their base organisation. They are: USA, Guatemala, El Salvador, Colombia, Bolivia, Chile, Haiti, Puerto Rico, Nicaragua, Brazil, Uruguay, Argentina, Northern Ireland, Eire, Holland, France, Spain, Portugal, Greece, Italy, West Germany, Turkey, Japan, Thailand, Philippines, Pakistan, Oman, Ethiopia, Malawi, Namibia, South Africa.

The PFLP was the group which initiated terrorism abroad; between 1968 and 1970 it was responsible for 25 terrorist actions, nearly all in Europe. Another group, Popular Front for the Liberation of Palestine – General Command (Ahmed Jibril) carried out the mid-air bombing of a Swiss airliner in February 1970. Following the expulsion of PLO terrorists from Jordan in 1970 Arafat's Fatah group turned to international terror and with PFLP created 'Black September'. Between 1971 and 1973 at least 60 international terror operations were carried out by Fatah-Black September, including the massacre of Israeli athletes at the 1972 Munich Olympics. Following President Sadat's journey to Jerusalem in November 1977 terrorist activity abroad increased; the major groups involved are Sa'iqa, backed by Syria, Iraqi-backed 'Black June' and the group led by Abu Nidal.

In Turkey throughout the 1970s terrorism was commonplace and thousands of political murders were committed. Under the rule of General Evren terrorism practically ceased and the democratic government restored in 1983 will be able to keep it suppressed for as long as it has the support of the army. Terrorist incidents took place in Cyprus while it was a British colony; after independence terrorism became commonplace because of the hostility between Greek Cypriots and Turkish Cypriots.

A few Jewish gangs practised terrorism against the British Army in the days before independence and resorted to counter-terror against the Arabs of Palestine but there has been very little Jewish terrorism since 1948.

Being an 'uninvolved bystander' is no protection against terrorism. Terrorist leaders, including George Habash of PFLP, have told me that there is no such thing as an innocent person. 'If you are alive you are involved,' he said. 'Your age, young or old, is of no consequence.' Nevertheless, the chances of a Western tourist or businessman becoming a terrorist victim are slight, though it should be remembered that European terror groups, including the IRA, have strong links with the PLO. Some young women, including English girls, have been picked up by Arab terrorists in Rome, Paris and other capitals and used as unwitting carriers of bombs, drugs and arms. In one incident two British girls agreed to carry a tape-recorder for some Arabs who had given them a good time in Rome. It contained a bomb which exploded in the hold of the aeroplane, though it was able to land safely.

See PALESTINE LIBERATION ORGANISATION: VIOLENCE: CIVIL WARS: ARAFAT

TIPPING

While it is best to get local advice on tipping some basic 'rules' exist. In Egypt tipping is universal for every kind of service but tips need never be large; for hotel staff, restaurants, cafés and bars the tip is usually 10 per cent of the bill. Throughout the Middle East hotels add a service charge, though this does not apply to Syria. Hairdressers usually expect 10 – 15 per cent of the bill but taxi-drivers do not expect a tip. This applies to Israel where, in addition, cloakroom attendants do not require a tip. Only in Egypt are cinema ushers tipped. If in doubt whether to tip or not it is better to tip but large amounts are not necessary. Tipping is quite different from bribery, q.v.

TRIBES

The tribal *system* has disintegrated in the Middle East and is to be found only among nomadic peoples but tribal *values* still exist. For instance, one of the most frequently asked questions is, 'What is your village.' The person questioned may live in a great city, such as Cairo or Damascus – or even in a European capital – but his tribal antecedents interest other Arabs or Turks or Iranians. It is important to know to what tribe a man belongs because you then know if he is potentially friend or foe or something in between.

In tribal society the role of the mediator in resolving conflict was always, and still is, crucial. In every conflict those involved feel that their honour is at stake and that to give in, even in the smallest way, would diminish their self-respect and dignity. To take the first step towards ending a dispute would be regarded as a sign of weakness. Hence it is impossible for an Arab to come to agreement in direct confrontation with an opponent. This tribal value and attitude is responsible for the difficulty in reaching compromise in disputes in Lebanon, among other places. Face-to-face encounter between adversaries is likely to aggravate the dispute – hence the need, as between tribes, for a mediator. Every Western visitor should always be careful not to criticise one Arab to another, for fear that the two have tribal connections.

Leila S. Kadi, writing about Arab summit conferences, notes that 'the divergence of interests among the Arab states can be traced back to the personal ambitions of some of the Arab rulers (Iraq, Jordan, Saudi Arabia) to extend their influence as much as possible at the expense of the other Arab states . . . This expresses quite well the medieval tribal mentality of their rulers.'
See HONOUR

TRUST

Trust between parties to a contract or between Muslims and non-Muslims is profoundly affected by Koranic injunctions. Chapter III states: 'Believers, do not make friends with any man other than your own people [fellow Muslims]. They will spare no pains to corrupt you. They desire nothing but your ruin. Their hatred is clear. . .' From this many Muslims infer that they cannot – indeed *should not* – trust Christians, Jews and others. In fact, many Middle Eastern businessmen often do trust their foreign counterparts and they themselves are often faithful to their contracts. However, when faced with trusting either a Muslim or non-Muslim, a Middle East Muslim person will choose the Muslim.

Some teachers and interpreters of the Koran say that no contract made by a Muslim with a non-Muslim is binding. For this reason it is important for Western businessmen to engage a specialist Islamic lawyer, preferably one practising in the West. Traditionally, a stranger or visitor could always trust his host to protect him but this tradition has been greatly weakened by the violence which has swept the Middle East in recent years. A man's allegiance is to his family and tribe and in continual factional fighting he can no longer guarantee his visitor's safety. It is most important for Western women to realise that they should never trust themselves to a Middle Eastern man; he sees women merely as sexual prey.

TUNISIA

Regarded as stable, forward-looking and pro-Western, Tunisia would appear to be one of the few Arab countries which does not have serious problems. But difficulties lie just beneath the surface, partly because of a sharp reduction in American and European development assistance.

Saudi Arabia, Kuwait and other Gulf states are concerned about the political consequences of the lack of Western money and are contributing, on a long-term basis, hundreds of millions of dollars to support Tunisia's economic and social plans. Tunisia has become a safe haven for the huge petrodollar surpluses of the oil producers but they have also good political reasons to transfer money there. Transfusions of money, the oil producers believe, could cure the ills of political opposition, social and economic unrest and Islamic

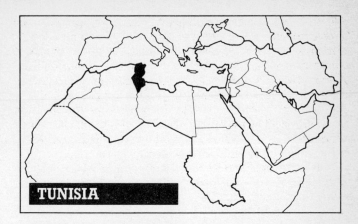

TUNISIA

fundamentalism similar to those which precipitated the Iran
revolution and the murder of Anwar Sadat of Egypt.

According to diplomats and bankers in Tunisia, the
moderate Arab states fear that should Tunisia fail to meet its
economic objectives it could erupt into chaos. This is
because the expectations of its highly politicised young and
aspiring class are so great that any check to national
prosperity would anger them. Already unemployment and
gross underemployment affect 28 per cent of the work
force. The population, 6·5 million in 1983, is growing too
rapidly.

The shift in US support from economic to military aid
reflects increasing tensions. Between 1972 and 1979
Tunisian arms purchases averaged less than $8 million a
year. In 1982 – 83 they exceeded $100 million.

Tunisia is worried about the danger of Libyan attacks,
perhaps in conjunction with internal unrest. President
Bourguiba is also concerned about the PLO contingent in
his country and its unsettling influence. The most insidious
threat of all comes from Iran whose mullahs consider that
Tunisia is too friendly with the West and therefore, they
say, the country is 'betraying Islam.'

Tunisia is relatively liberal and probably the most
'cultured' of Middle East countries, largely because of the
influence of the French who once 'owned' it. Islam is the

official and majority religion and Sunnis are the predominant sect; there are Christian and Jewish minorities. While Arabic is the official language French is widely spoken, especially in education, commerce and administration; three of the five national newspapers are in French. English is spoken in business circles as well.

Despite a degree of social liberalism, absolute political power is held by the president and the prime minister whom he appoints. The National Assembly is elected from a list of the single party, the Parti Socialiste Destourien.

With an area of 163,610 sq. km. Tunisia offers much to the tourist, with mountains, a long sandy coastline, several large oases and many historic sites.

See ISLAMIC REVOLUTION

TURKEY

Turkey, after Egypt, the most populous country of the Middle East, with an estimated 45 million people, is extremely powerful militarily, with regular forces of 600,000 and reserves of another 500,000. Sitting astride the only outlet from the Black Sea, bridging West and East and dominating the north-east Mediterranean, it has great strategic importance. Most of Turkey's population are Sunni Muslims but the country is not Islamic; Kemal Ataturk,

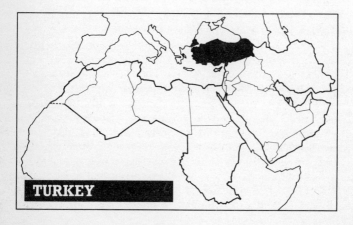

TURKEY

president from 1922 until 1938, blamed the Islamic religion
for Turkey's backwardness. He replaced Islamic legal codes
by Western models, secularised education, ordered that the
Arab alphabet was to be superseded by Latin characters,
and barred the fez because it was a symbol of the wearer's
attachment to Islam and because he considered it
demeaning.

Between 1960 and 1979 Turkey was beset by numerous
economic and social problems. In the former year the army
threw out the government and executed Prime Minister
Menderes and some of his cabinet. A new constitution
provided for a bicameral legislature and judicial curbs on
government power. The hope that these new institutions
would produce a stable and effective government was not
fulfilled. Between 1961 and 1980 there were 19 governments, most of them flimsy coalitions.

Anti-Turkish diplomatic activity by the Soviet Union had
driven Turkey into the Western camp and it entered NATO
in 1952 and the Baghdad Pact (later named CENTO) in
1955. These alliances brought in much Western money,
particularly from the USA. Nothing, however, could solve
Turkey's intractable dispute with Greece, especially over
Cyprus. Turkey's right to Cyprus and to Aegean oil is the
one issue on which all Turkey's parties agree.

In 1971 the military again removed a Prime Minister,
Suleiman Demirel, but restored full civilian government in
1973. During the seventies terrorism became endemic in
Turkey, with right-wing, left-wing and Islamic extremists
all murdering indiscriminately. In December 1978 fierce
fighting broke out in the town of Kahramanmaras and 150
people were killed. The world had ignored other violent
events in Turkey but the Kahramanmaras crisis alerted the
international community to the nation's precarious
situation. The violence was aimed at Alevi Shi'a Turks,
possibly because Sunni Muslims, worried about the collapse
of the Shah's regime in Iran, feared a threat from other
Shi'a extremists. Martial law was declared in most of
Turkey's provinces.

In 1980 General Evren and a party of high-ranking
officers dissolved parliament, banned all political parties

and ruled by decree. Democratic government was dead but the country became more peaceful and stable. Civilian government was restored after free elections in November 1983 though General Evren allowed only three parties to contest them. He and his group retain significant supervisory control. Turkey probably represents the Middle East's most successful attempt at parliamentary government but some Turks conclude that the experiment in multiparty democracy was premature. Basically pro-Western and anxious to take part in Western institutions, including the EEC, Turkey is vulnerable to Islamic extremists. The Iranians want to see Turkey brought back to Islam; that is, they plan to destroy its secular nature. This is not likely to happen but the extremists could bring about another reign of terror.

Many Western tourists visit Turkey, mostly from France, West Germany and Britain, and despite differences in culture they generally find the atmosphere more relaxed than in the Arab countries. Begging is prohibited and harassment of foreign tourists is punished. The easiest way to get into an argument in Turkey is to say anything complimentary about Greece.

Turkey has a diverse society, with a large educated and sophisticated class in the cities and millions of poor, ignorant peasants in Anatolia. In the distant regions of this large country – 780,576 sq. km. – there is distrust and dislike of foreigners bordering on xenophobia but visitors are freely accepted in the resort areas. Foreign businessmen find the Turks honourable partners in trade; corruption, though present, is less blatant than in many other countries.

See TERRORISM: SOVIET UNION IN THE MIDDLE EAST: UNITED STATES IN THE MIDDLE EAST

UNITED ARAB EMIRATES _____

The UAE came into being in 1971 when seven small emirates combined to give themselves a stronger political and economic voice. They are Abu Dhabi, Dubai, Sharjah, Ajman, Umm al-Quwainm, Ras al-Khaimah and Fujairah and collectively they have an area of 77,830 sq. km. Only 25

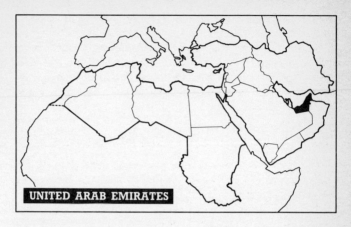

UNITED ARAB EMIRATES

per cent of the population of 900,000 are indigenous and most Arabs are of the Sunni sect, though there are smaller communities of Shi'a Muslims, Christians and Hindus. Apart from many non-UAE Arabs, there are Indians, Pakistanis, Baluchis and Iranians; in the larger cities live sizeable communities of Western expatriates.

The Head of State is also the ruler of Abu Dhabi, Sheikh Zayed bin Sultan al-Nahayan, while the Vice-President and Prime Minister is the ruler of Dubai, Sheikh Rashid bin Saeed al-Maktoum. The UAE, despite its collective nature, is classed as a constitutional monarchy. The Supreme Council – the seven rulers of the respective emirates – elects the president-ruler. The president appoints the prime minister and cabinet; there is also a 40-member Federal National Council, all of whose members are appointed, which acts as a legislative body.

The stability of the UAE is by no means certain; the Iranian upheaval is too close for comfort. Dubai alone has 30,000 Iranian nationals, deeply under the influence of the ayatollahs across the Gulf. They are playing on the existing tensions among the seven rulers, some of whom resent and fear the power of the two biggest states, Abu Dhabi and Dubai. They do have one thing in common – all depend on Saudi Arabia to support the UAE armed forces of 25,000 in an emergency. Prosperous from oil money and international banking, the UAE are generous donors of aid; they provide about $1·4 billion in loans, grants and contributions annually. The importance of Middle East ambassadors in business matters can be seen through some of the vast sums reported to have been paid by certain British and American companies as commission on contracts awarded in the UAE.

UNITED STATES IN THE MIDDLE EAST _____

The Americans have had a direct interest in the Middle East only since the establishment of the state of Israel, which the Americans support. With arms and money the USA has given the Israelis protection against their Arab enemies. The USA has never been anti-Arab nor has it sought to dominate the Arab world; indeed until the British withdrew from the Middle East in the 1950s and 1960s the Americans had no real policy for the Middle East other than the general intention of preventing the Soviet Union from gaining too much influence. Since 1973 this has dictated policy; almost everything the USA does is designed to pre-empt Soviet actions or takes the form of a reaction to such actions.

Above all, the USA wishes to maintain peace in the Gulf because much of its oil is exported to the USA and its NATO allies. The Americans have been inept in their Middle East activities, largely because their confidence exceeds their knowledge. They did not foresee the downfall of the Shah in 1979 and the consequent Iranian Revolution; they suffered great humiliation when their Teheran embassy was taken over and the staff held hostage. The particular points on which the USA has taken a definite stand are these:

- Military and financial aid for Egypt as a 'reward' for having made peace with Israel; in fact, the USA gives the Egyptians only a little less money than Israel.

- Support for the 'lawful' Lebanese government against the Syrians, whose army occupies much of the country, and against their Russian backers.

- Declaration of pax Americana for the Gulf by using a powerful fleet in the Indian Ocean and shore bases in some of the small Gulf states.

- Continuing support for Israel's right to exist.

- Financial and other aid for any country which might fall to Communism or to Soviet influence if it did not get this aid. Recipient countries are Tunisia, Morocco, Sudan.

- Powerful military support to Turkey because, as a NATO member, Turkey blocks the Soviet Union from easy access to the Mediterranean.

There is little to suggest that the Carter or Reagan administrations had any real understanding of Arab and Islamic attitudes and values. Recent American history in the Middle East is littered with misjudgements and calamities. The Americans were shocked when the Saudis refused to endorse the Egypt–Israel peace treaty; there was never any possibility that this would happen.

See ISLAM: SOVIET UNION IN THE MIDDLE EAST: individual countries

VENGEANCE

It is axiomatic in Middle East society that an injury done to a man's honour must be avenged, or else he becomes permanently dishonoured. And, of course, there is the sexual honour of the woman, through which her entire paternal family is constantly and dangerously exposed to the possibility of becoming dishonoured. Should her 'honour' be tarnished vengeance must follow. Revenge or vengeance is fundamental in this situation though it is directed more against the woman than against the seducer.

One of the oldest heritages of the Arabs – many scholars consider it to be pre-Islamic – is *lex talionis*, the law of retaliation. This it not only left to the individual and his immediate kin group to take revenge for any injury suffered but made it their *duty* under penalty of forfeiting their honour. This law is evident in the still current Arab saying *Dam butlub dam* (Blood demands blood).

Blood feuds are not confined to the Arab world; they feature in other Mediterranean cultural traditions as well. But it is among Arabs that the blood feud has remained a most important and emphatic value. Inevitably every homicide, premeditated or accidental, gives rise to blood revenge and triggers a chain reaction that soon involves an increasing number of men and groups. This is why we see so much bloodshed in modern times in Lebanon, Syria, Iraq, Algeria and Iran. With possibly 100,000 people killed in Lebanon between the years 1975 and 1985 revenge must go on for generations and, of course, every act of revenge calls for counter-vengeance. President Nasser made clear the need for vengeance on March 3, 1955, when he said, 'We (the Arabs) are a people that never forgets if it has been injured, but the injury to us increases our determination and our stubbornness.'

While individual revenge in most societies, and especially in urban environments, has greatly decreased, national revenge has been heightened by nationalism itself. Syrian politicians, for instance, consider it necessary to continue to fight Israel until they have achieved revenge for military humiliations in 1967, 1973 and 1982. Iranians have the same attitude towards the Iraqis.

Islam, through the Koran, prescribes rules for retaliation. In his translation and commentary on the Koran, A. Yusuf Ali[28] states, 'Islam says that if you must take a life for a life, at least there should be some measure of equality in it; the killing of the slave of a tribe should not involve a blood feud where many free men would be killed . . .' Elsewhere the Koran states that an injury committed in retaliation should not exceed the injury committed in the first place.

Vengeance and retaliation are still prominent in Turkish attitudes, and in rural communities this attitude is not only accepted but expected. Iran, under Khomeini, has become a vengeful society because the mullahs, who dominate the people, preach revenge against those 'enemies of God' who, the mullahs say, have exploited the Iranian people. When

the exiled Shah died of cancer the Iranians had a national
day of prayer – in *praise* of his death.
See HONOUR: PRIDE: WOMEN: TRIBES: FAMILY: SHI'A ISLAM

VIOLENCE

In Middle Eastern culture, violence, anger and aggression
flare readily; all are condoned by society and readily forgiven. People go on a rampage and their rage becomes quite
irrational. The traditional nature of violence is indicated by
the Arab writer Fawaz Turki.[29] 'His (the Arab's)
consciousness is stuffed and devastated by images of
violence – violence that a Palestinian particularly grows up
with like he grows up with his skin.' T.E. Lawrence said of
the Syrians: 'From childhood they are lawless, obeying
their fathers only from physical fear.' The great Jordanian
scholar, Aref el-Aref, considered that 'Violence is bred into
the Jordanian by his mother and nurtured by every adult he
encounters.' 'Violence,' a Libyan cabinet minister told me
in 1973, 'is the Muslim's most positive form of prayer.'
  Through television, the world has seen mass displays of
violence, notably in Teheran, involving millions of people,
mostly males. Violence can be directed against other people,
buildings, vehicles and aircraft. Amazingly, once an
outburst runs its course sincere contrition often follows. I
have seen Arabs and Iranians baffled by what they have
done hours before and quite unable to explain why they did
it. Professional rabble-rousers can quickly bring a crowd to
the point of violence. In Cairo in April 1956, near the
university, I saw a lone man stand on a ladder and begin a
tirade against the British. Within moments he had a small
audience and it grew to a thousand in minutes. In 15
minutes the crowd was screaming and shouting and
marching against the British Embassy. In Tripoli in July
1973 I watched government agents round up peaceable
workmen and bring them to the British Embassy by truck.
Outside the embassy the agents goaded the workmen into a
frenzy and they rampaged into the building and caused a lot
of damage. When they departed their anger had evaporated

and they were relaxed and laughing. In a bazaar violence can erupt in seconds over some disagreement.

Western visitors who see a crowd gathering should quickly take themselves away. Even if only two men start to fight it is wise to leave the place at once. When caught up in a violent demonstration it is best to work your way out of the mob and into a side street or into a building. However, I have sometimes found it impossible to extricate myself from the crush; then the best course is to offer to join the demonstration by waving your fist and shouting. You will draw less attention to yourself this way than by keeping passive. A journalist friend, in Amman, kept shouting 'Rule Britannia!' while those around him were calling for Anthony Eden's death and their shouting buried his.

See FATE: SOCIETY: FANATICISM

WAR

The difference in attitudes to war in the Western world and war in the Middle East is that the West sees it as a last resort, when every diplomatic channel has been exhausted. In the Islamic world, war, rebellion and insurrection are 'normal' means of settling a dispute.

Since 1945, when World War II ended, not one of all the countries which make up the Middle East has been without war or internal unrest so serious that it constitutes a form of war. Arab hostility towards Israel has meant that this country has hardly known peace since its foundation as a state in 1948. But this particular hostility never has been the main cause of instability in the Middle East; the greater number of wars have had no connection with Israel.

Western visitors to the Middle East can always expect to hear talk of war, whether it is of a war past, present or projected. It is one of the main topics of conversation and an insistent pre-occupation. This is understandable since the region is the most war-prone in the world. In chronological order these are some of the principal wars:

| 1945 | Iran: Rebellion in Azerbaijan |
| 1946 | Iran: Rebellion in southern provinces |

1946	Iraq: Uprising in Kurdistan
1947 – 49	Israel: War against Israel by five Arab nations
1949	Lebanon: Rebellion suppressed
1952 – 59	Cyprus: Guerrilla warfare
1952	Tunisia: Uprising against French rule
1952	Saudi Arabian invasion of Buraimi Oasis against Sultan of Muscat and Oman
1953 – 56	Israel: Intermittent frontier clashes
1953	Morocco: Uprising against the Sultan
1953 – 55	Guerrilla operations throughout Morocco
1954 – 62	Algeria: War of Independence against France compounded with civil war
1956 – 82	Israel: Terrorist War against Israel by PLO factions
1956	Sinai Campaign: Israel pre-empts invasion by Egypt, Syria and Jordan; Britain and France involved
1957	Morocco: War against Spain
1957	Revolt in Muscat and Oman
1958	Iraq: Officer revolt, overthrow of monarchy
1958	Lebanon: Insurrection inspired by Syria and Egypt suppressed
1958 – 61	Tunisia: Hostilities against France
1959 – 66	Sudan: Civil war of northern Arabs against southern Negro Christians. 1,000,000 negroes killed
1951 – 65	Yemen: Egypt's war with Yemen; Yemen Civil War
1963	Algeria: Border war with Morocco
1963	Sudan: Further rebellion in southern Sudan
1963	Iraqi revolt
1963 – 64	Cyprus: Civil War
1964	Cyprus: Attacks by Turkey
1965 – 67	Aden: British war against rebels
1965 – 70	Yemen: Civil War with Egyptian involvement
1967	Israel: 'Six-Day War' pre-empts attack by Egypt, Syria and Jordan
1967 – 70	Cyprus: Civil War
1969 – 73	Suez Canal: War of attrition between Egypt and Israel

1970	Jordan: 'Civil War'; PLO terrorists forced out
1970	Jordan: Syrian Invasion
1972	Yemen: Civil War
1973	Yom Kippur War against Israel by Syria and Egypt; known as 'the Great Crossing' in Egypt. At least nine Arab states and at least four non-Middle East states actively aided the Egyptian-Syrian war effort
1975	Cyprus: Turkish invasion
1975 – 85	Libya: Intermittent wars in Chad
1975 – 82	Somalia: War against Ethiopia
1975 – 85	Eritrean Revolt against Ethiopia
1975 – 76	Syrian-Iraq Confrontation
1975 – 76	Lebanon: Civil War (It was still continuing in 1985)
1976 – 85	Morocco: War against Polisario Movement in Southern Sahara
1978 – 85	Iran: War against the Kurds
1978 – 79	Iran: Islamic Revolution
1979 – 85	Iran-Iraq: The Gulf War
1982	Lebanon: Israel's 'Operation Peace for Galilee' against PLO terrorists in southern Lebanon.
1983	Syria: Civil War against Muslim Brotherhood
1984 – 85	Sudan: Civil War

This list does not take into account the persistent attacks by Iran and Iraq on Kurdish dissidents, the numerous incursions by Libyan troops into neighbouring countries, the border conflicts between Morocco and Algeria, internal coups and such incidents as the Islamic revolutionaries attack on the Great Mosque of Mecca in 1979.

WEST BANK

Every Western reader of almost any newspaper has frequently come across the term 'the West Bank' and all the controversy associated with it. Every Christian tourist to the Holy Land will visit the West Bank, since here are some of the holy places of Christendom, such as Bethlehem and the River Jordan. The loosely used label is of modern origin and refers to the west bank of the Jordan. Throughout the Mandate period, when Britain was responsible for governing the region, it was known by its historical names of Samaria, in the north and Judea, in the south. The expression 'West Bank' has little meaning in either of the countries associated with it in modern times, Jordan and Israel.

Its recent history is briefly explained. The Jordan River was the frontier between Palestine and Transjordan after Britain truncated Palestine in 1922. Mandatory Palestine, as recognised by the League of Nations, consisted of the entire territory that now comprises the State of Israel, the *East Bank* of the Jordan and the Hashemite Kingdom of Jordan. In 1922 the British arbitrarily stated that Transjordan – that is *across* the Jordan on the east side – could not be settled by Jews. This left them only 23 per cent of the area of the Mandate, that territory west of the Jordan. Legally, Transjordan remained part of Mandatory Palestine and British rule continued until 1947, when the formal partition of Palestine between Jews and Arabs occurred. In 1948 King Abdullah's Arab Legion invaded Western Palestine (now the West Bank) and the Old City of Jerusalem, the centre of Judaism. It was at this point that Abdullah began to call the captured land the West Bank. His nation, Transjordan, formally annexed the West Bank in 1950, changing its name and that of the nation as a whole to Jordan.

Under the partition resolution, the West Bank had been allocated to the proposed new Arab state so West Bank Palestinians opposed Jordan's takeover. Only two governments, Britain and Pakistan, recognised the annexation *de jure*. The USA never recognised Jordan's annexation *de jure*, or Jordan's sovereignty over the Old City of Jerusalem. On July 29, 1977, Secretary of State Cyrus Vance said, 'It is an open question as to who has legal right to the West Bank.' Legally, it is unallocated territory. In the 1967 'Six-Day War' Israel captured the West Bank and in recent years about 30,000 Jews have settled on it in tiny villages.

The principal towns of the West Bank are Nablus,

Ramallah, Hebron and Jenin and here the Palestinians live. While most are Sunni Muslim there are pockets of Arab Christians. Generally the West Bank Palestinians are better educated than those in Jordan and mostly they are a peaceful industrious people but occasionally they demonstrate against the Israeli military presence on the West Bank, as well as against the small Jewish settlements. For many years the West Bank was the base from which the PLO launched its terrorist attacks against Israel; this is the reason given for the Israeli occupation. West Bank people, while resenting the Israeli presence, admit that they are better off than under Jordanian rule. For instance, the West Bank had no universities while under Jordanian administration but now has four. Many of the population of 726,000 go to work in Israel itself.

See JORDAN: ISRAEL: PALESTINE LIBERATION ORGANISATION: TERRORISM

WOMEN

To prepare for the celebration of International Women's Day in 1967 the Algerian newspaper *El Moujahid* opened its columns to readers' views on the topic. Nearly all were from men and many were too obscene to be published. Among the more acceptable comments were these:

> The Algerian woman's participation in the revolution of the nation is a catastrophe for the Muslim religion and a betrayal of the Koran. Allow me to say that the debauchery and the confusions in the present administration are due to women. Our socialism rests on the pillars of Islam, not on the emancipation of the woman with her make-up, her coiffure, her finery, which causes unbridled passions to burst forth; the effect of these passions is detrimental to humanity as a whole causing discord and quarrelling, the crimes which are generally caused by women.

> The Koran itself is not unkind to women but it is patronising, offering them protection along with orphans, imbeciles and other feeble-minded persons. On women's

behaviour the Koran states, (Ch. 24), 'And tell the believing women to lower their gaze and be modest, and to display of their adornment only that which is apparent, and to draw their veils over their bosoms, and not to reveal their adornment save to their own husbands or fathers or husband's fathers or their sons or their husband's sons . . . or their male attendants who lack vigour . . . (being castrated).' The Koran explicitly states that men are superior to women, it admonishes women to obey their husbands and it advises men to beat their women 'and send them to their beds apart' if they misbehave or fail to obey. The practices of veiling, seclusion and general social segregation of the sexes have helped to maintain two quite different societies in the Islamic Middle East – the world of men and the world of women.

The complex situation is partly brought about by the upbringing of the Arab and Persian boy. He is constantly told – and has the evidence of what he sees – that males are superior to females. A boy can beat his sisters with impunity and, in many Arab groups, his mother.

Dr Sayyid Uwaya,[30] adviser to the Egyptian National Centre for Social and Criminal Research, has listed 20 reasons for women's low status. They include:

- A woman marries only in order to serve her husband.

- Egyptian women are not allowed to take important jobs.

- In many cases the Egyptian woman is forced to marry. She can be divorced if she does not bear male children but she herself has no right to divorce.

- The male child is preferred by the parents.

- The term 'woman' is regarded as a pejorative one, and is even used as an insult or a curse.

- Women are considered to be lacking in intelligence and religion.

- On marriage a woman loses her identity and even her name; she is merely 'the wife of Ahmed' or 'the mother of Rahman'. Further, she is inferior to her sons.

- The percentage of illiteracy among females is extremely high; in some villages it is just under 100 per cent.

Even among the best Arab novelists, women are merely sex objects. Arab male novelists include female characters for no other purpose than to create sex situations. Women constitute less than 8 per cent of the work force in most Middle East countries. While men work in modern industry women cluster in the more casual and lower-paid occupations such as domestic service and petty trade where they form a pool of underemployed surplus labour.

No shortage of male labour exists so the training and education of women is given low priority. Given the absence of social services and modern household appliances in most areas, women's domestic labour includes care of the old and infirm as well as of the children and the laborious processing of raw materials for family consumption. The only professions where women are found in any numbers are teaching, medicine and nursing.

Since 1960 an increasing number of Arab writers, teachers and doctors, influenced by their experience in Western countries, have been protesting against the injustices and cruelties inflicted on Arab women but the emancipation of women – the real revolution in Arab society – has yet to come. Even in the relatively enlightened countries women are far from emancipated. For instance, in Egypt a man is legally permitted to beat a disobedient wife. In Lebanon abortion is punishable with imprisonment. In Kuwait women have no vote. In Jordan polygamy is permitted.

The unmarried woman, living apart from her family, is a rarity; less than 2 per cent of Middle Eastern women remain single and most divorcees remarry. Other than in Egypt and Lebanon there is no feminist movement and even in Egypt it is the province of middle and upper class women, and their preoccupation with legal reform and birth control gives them little time for an integrated approach to women's status in social and economic terms. In some countries, such as Saudi Arabia, women have no public place whatever and are rarely allowed to leave their homes.

Within the Palestinian movement women do have some rights. They are encouraged to participate in the revolution, to work, to carry arms, to debate policies. The effect on women's roles and status has been great but two facts must be noted: Very few women hold the high-level political positions; the best known female symbol of 'resistance' is the 'mother of martyrs'. Also, workshops and training programmes developed for women stress needlework and other textile crafts. In South Yemen some of the same conditions exist. Only in Tunisia are women given legal equality.

Women are not equal sexual partners. As a lover the Arab male is generally violent and often cruel. His suspicions about the chastity of his womenfolk – to him women are naturally immoral if given the chance – make him neurotic. The frequent attacks on unescorted Western women working in Arab countries are explained by the Arab's conviction that they lack the moral standards imposed by society on Arab women and are therefore fair game.

In the absence of a feminist lobby much is left to the very few Arab women with enough education, independence and status to speak openly about injustice. The Palestinian, Soraya Antonius,[31] made a bold statement in 1979:

> Women suffer from the social harassment and legal harassment imposed in every Arab country. The relevant laws are:
> a) The 'honour' law provisions which in effect condone the murder of a woman by her husband or any male related to her if she is suspected or accused of illicit sexual relations with a man.
> b) The divorce laws.
> c) The law which forbids a woman to travel outside the country without written permission from her husband or other male guardian.
> First of all we need legal equality, so that a man can be imprisoned for divorcing his wife just because she's a militant, or for beating her because she has joined the Women's Union.

Even among Westernised Arabs, women are considered unreliable, prone to sin and unintelligent compared with men. The plight of women is vividly described by Dr Ian Young in his book *The Private Life of Islam*.[32] Dr Young, who worked in an Algerian hospital, particularly reveals the misery of women in Algerian society.

See FAMILY: KORAN: LAW: LOVE AND SEX: MARRIAGE

YEMEN ARAB REPUBLIC

This is North Yemen, the country whose civil war between 1962 and 1970 drew in Egypt because Nasser saw it as a way of extending his power into the Arabian peninsula. Since 1970 the country has returned to tribal power, with strong Saudi influence aimed at controlling both the government and the major tribes. One president, Ibrahim al Hamdi, was assassinated in 1977 and his successor, Ahmed al Ghashmi, died in June 1978 when a booby-trapped briefcase blew up in his office. The position of the present president, Ali Abdullah Saleh, is precarious and assassination attempts are reported almost monthly.

With a population of 7·2 million, the YAR has armed forces totalling 21,550, largely armed by the USA ($500 million worth of equipment during the Reagan administration). Executions of dissidents occur frequently. While virtually all inhabitants are Muslim, there is a marked split. In the north are the Zaidis, a Shi'a sect, and in the south and along the Red Sea coast the Shafis, a Sunni sect. Agriculturally the YAR is the wealthiest area of the Arabian peninsula because its mountains receive between 16

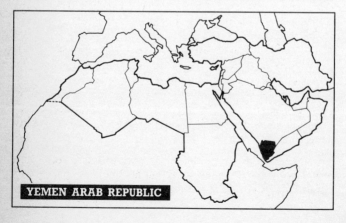

YEMEN ARAB REPUBLIC

and 35 inches of rain a year; this provides water for irrigation, though this is not as developed as it could be.

The YAR has no railways and only 750 km. of good roads in all its 200,000 sq. km. No long-distance routes other than air are recommended for Western visitors. Nevertheless, North Yemen is opening up to more and more tourists. Most follow a triangular circuit between Sana'a, the capital, Taiz and Hodeida but archaeological sites abound and some, like Marib, are easily reached from Sana'a. This is, after all, the fabled land of the Queen of Sheba. It is a punishable offence to excavate in YAR and even picking up bits of broken pottery is dangerous and can anger local tribesmen who may be watching at a distance.

Medical facilities are poor; visitors should be prepared for gastric upsets and must avoid untreated water. Malaria is endemic in parts of YAR.

YEMEN PEOPLE'S DEMOCRATIC REPUBLIC _____

Better known as South Yemen, and a Marxist state despite its 'democratic' label, the YPDR includes the former British colony of Aden. The Yemenis fought a war of independence against Britain, which withdrew in 1967. A country of 388,000 sq. km., the YPDR has a population of only 2 million, most of them with tribal affiliations.

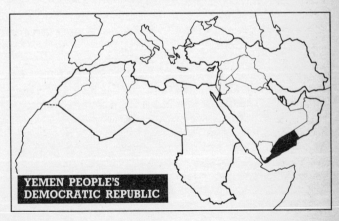

YEMEN PEOPLE'S
DEMOCRATIC REPUBLIC

Violence is endemic. In 1966 Ali Hussein Kadi, president of the Aden Council of Labour Federations, was murdered; his death was followed by that of Miakkram Ghaleb, general secretary of Aden's al-Umah Party. In February 1967 a former minister, Said Muhammad, was murdered and in 1970, Faisal Sha'abi, a former prime minister, was shot 'while attempting to escape from his detention camp.' In March 1970, 40 opposition leaders were invited to attend discussions with the government and all were killed at the meeting. In 1978 the chairman of the Presidential Council, Salem Ali Rubayyi, and two of his ministers were executed in a coup. The country is controlled by the Yemeni Socialist Party, whose leader is Abdul Fattah Ismail. He, like most of the population, is a Sunni Muslim of the Shafi sect.

South Yemen is one of the poorest Arab countries, since it has no substantial natural resources. Strongly pro-Soviet Union, the country depends on the Russians for aid. After 1975 Libya also provided money because the South Yemen government opposed the Saudi Arabian monarchy, which the Libyan president regards as 'anti-Islamic'. With 70 per cent adult illiteracy, the YPDR is backward but there is some hope for the future. For instance, in 1967 there were only 1,750 teachers; now there are 9,500. Over 200 doctors are practising and half of them are Yemeni. Other social measures include a ban on the chewing of the narcotic *qat* except on Thursday afternoons and Fridays. Women have been granted greater rights though they are still inadequate. Through legislation and ideological appeal the population's tribal identifications are being reduced.

The YPDR has armed forces of 25,500, including 18,000 conscripts, armed and financed by the Soviet Union. Most of the military aircraft are flown by Russian and Cuban crews. The country has been a base for Arab and international terrorist training, especially on the island of Socotra in the Red Sea. Relations with North Yemen, Saudi Arabia and Oman are always tense. Because of Soviet influence, there is considerable anti-Western sentiment in South Yemen and foreign visitors need to be cautious.

ZIONISM _____

Zionism was born in the 1880s as the movement which was to give national liberation to the Jewish people. In practice, it meant a return to their homeland in the Middle East. The word itself comes from the symbolic hill, Zion, on which King David lived in ancient Jerusalem; Mount Zion still exists in Jerusalem.

Zionism was brought into political being by the Jewish journalist Theodor Herzl in a pamphlet called *The Jewish State*. He did not invent Zionism but he was the first to make it clear to the world. The Zionist Organisation which Herzl founded undertook the practical work in Palestine and created the basic instruments – a bank and a fund to buy land for the farmers who would come to join those Jews who had been there for generations. Ethical and utopian idealists, the Zionists were convinced that the Jewish state would be realised only by manual labour, idealism and sacrifice.

The rebirth of the State of Israel in 1948 after a struggle waged by three trail-blazing generations of pioneers, first in the ideological domain alone, and then in the practical spheres of production and defence, marked the climax of the movement.

The Zionist movement works through two parallel bodies. One is the World Zionist Organization, with its executive in Jerusalem; the Executive is headed by the Zionist Congress which meets every four years and all Jewish communities are represented. The second body is the Jewish Agency, charged with implementing Zionism's tasks.

Zionism is indifferent to race or colour as a factor in shaping the character and ethos of Israeli society. A majority of the population of Israel is in fact dark-skinned and the Israelis have never discriminated against people with black skins nor have they prized a lighter skin.

Israelis have never attached any significance to mystical doctrines of race-purity or to the notion of 'superior' and 'inferior' races. Such doctrines, which presuppose a belief in higher hereditary qualities, and the virtues of the blood, are alien to Zionism and to Judaism.

The President of Senegal, Leopold Senghor, has described Zionism – together with Arabism and Negritude – as *'le message des peuples souffrants'* (the message of suffering nations). Zionism, a Jewish writer has said, is 'the secular messianism of the Jewish people, the longest suffering victims of oppression and racism. Like other authentic national movements, it is ultimately a return to the sources and original identity of the Jewish people and the recovery of their human dignity.'

The Zionist movement misjudged the intensity of Palestinian Arab opposition to its idealistic aims. Any Western visitor who becomes involved in discussion with Arabs about Israel will hear people say, 'We don't object to the Jews only to the Zionists.' This makes no linguistic or political sense. Not all Israelis are card-carrying Zionists but every Israeli subscribes to the Zionist belief that Jews have an inalienable right to the Land of Israel. To object to one Jew in Israel is to object to all.

See JEWS: JERUSALEM: JUDAISM

A CHECK LIST OF DANGERS, RISKS, PROHIBITIONS AND BEHAVIOUR _____

Never say anything critical about the Prophet Muhammad, even in jest. It can lead to expulsion from an Islamic country, even to attack and murder.

Never expect any action to be private, no matter how discreet you imagine you are being. This applies particularly to sexual adventures; Arab men watch over not only their own women but other men's women and they can do nothing that is unobserved.

In the same way, do not expect business dealings to be kept private, though this may happen if your Middle East partner wishes to conceal the fact that he has taken a bribe.

Always find out the religious affiliation – Shi'a, Sunni, Maronite, Greek Orthodox and so on – before you go far with an acquaintanceship. Do not be drawn into comment about religion until you know the religion of your companion.

Avoid smiling at a woman in the house of your host; she will be in trouble for having 'incited' you. And do not thank her for your meal. If her husband thinks that thanks are warranted, *he* will thank her on your behalf.

Do not offer to shake hands with a woman or girl.

It is dangerous to show too much money in public; this makes you a marked man for thieves.

Never expect an appointment to be kept punctually.

Do not expect to be thanked for a gift. Thanks are due to Allah and you are merely Allah's instrument in bringing the present.

Houses with blue doors are generally brothels; Middle East prostitutes are usually diseased.

Helpful boys are often male prostitutes. Also diseased.

No Arab likes to say 'No' to a request for an interview, to an invitation to lunch or to a request for permission to do something or other. The absence of a refusal does not necessarily mean that he assents or agrees. If he fails to keep an appointment, does not respond to your telephone messages, does not send the document you require and generally wastes your time it should be assumed that he is not interested in pursuing the matter, whatever it is.

Wherever she goes in Arab lands a woman needs a male escort; even a five-year-old boy will do. No 'respectable' woman appears alone in public.

An Arab tells you what he believes you want to hear. In the same way, the word is the deed in the Middle East; when a man promises his help he has already given it. It is usually necessary for the Western visitor to remind him of his promise. In contrast, an Israeli means what he says – sometimes uncompromisingly so.

It is discourteous to eat pork when dining with a Jew.

When visiting an Arab Muslim never compliment the woman of the house on her home or anything in it; everything belongs to her husband. In any case many a host will feel obliged to give his guest something that he has praised and this can be embarrassing.

Do not proffer your left hand to a Muslim; it is 'unclean'.

In Israel do not tell Jewish jokes unless you know your companion intimately. Jews like jokes – but they prefer to do the telling.

Remember that alcohol is forbidden to Muslims and that in most parts of the Middle East visitors may drink it only in the privacy of a hotel room. Israelis drink little alcohol and it is forbidden in the armed forces.

Should you hire a self-drive car give way on the road to the local driver, regardless of whether he is on your right or left or in front. The most dangerous places for driving are Cairo (where drivers are best described as maniacal), Tel Aviv (suicidal), Istanbul (homicidal) and Algiers (reckless).

Try to avoid using public transport throughout the Middle East as it is grossly overcrowded and uncomfortable. If you travel on an

Israeli bus sit down quickly or get a good grip on some support; the drivers have all the finesse of tank drivers. A reasonable and inexpensive form of transport is the shared taxi, which is common throughout the Middle East.

Even when visiting an Arab country for some official occasion, such as a trade fair, the Western businessman or journalist should not assume that all will go smoothly. Organisations and individuals will have been appointed to help the visitors but in some matters they are ineffectual. On such occasions there is often an assurance that 'tours will be arranged.' More often than not nothing will be arranged. The visitor will then wish to rent a car to do his own touring. The degree of difficulty varies with the country. In some countries the visitor will need, even when dealing through Avis, his British driving licence, his passport, xeroxes of the country's visa or stamps inside the passport, and a letter in Arabic from a local sponsor. Then there is the eye test, which can only be taken at the police station, which may be closed. The eye test is nothing like a Western optician's test. In the United Arab Emirates the test chart is made up entirely of what looks like Es, some lying on their backs and others back to front. Not that it matters – the test can generally be passed by making a contribution to the police benevolent fund. Even then the licence may not be ready until the day after you are due to leave the country but if the Avis agent is efficient, and he generally is, you will probably get a car anyway. There are still problems, especially in the newly rich countries; they have built many dual-carriage roads but have no maps for them. A further problem is that some roads just end suddenly in the desert. On the whole, it is better to find an expatriate countryman and induce him to take you on a tour.

It is usual for private cars to give lifts to soldiers in Israel and it is safe for a visitor to do this.

Be very careful where you eat and ask advice on restaurants from fastidious local friends.

In Cyprus be very sure whether you are talking to a Greek or a Turk. Most British residents of Cyprus prefer the Turks because, the expatriates say, the Turks are less bombastic and more trustworthy.

Before you enter a mosque – which you may safely do – take off your shoes. Women must wear a decorous dress and cover their arms before entering any holy place. This also applies to the Baha'i temple.

Before a man enters a synagogue or approaches the Western (Wailing) Wall in Jerusalem – which he may safely do – he must cover his head.

Few holy places will admit a man wearing shorts; the Israeli guards at the entrance to Christian and Muslim places of worship will turn you away if you are so dressed.

Remember that Friday is the holy day for Muslims and Saturday – which means from sunset on Friday to sunset on Saturday – is the Jews' holy day. It is essential to stay out of Orthodox suburbs and towns on these days.

Any transaction which could be completed in an hour or even in minutes in the West will take many hours and even days in the Middle East, except in Israel and the cosmopolitan parts of Turkey.

You will often be asked your religion. It is better to say simply 'Christian' (if this is the case) rather than give details of your Lutheran, Anglican, Roman Catholic or Baptist background. This confuses Middle East people.

As a woman, be prepared to be ignored by men in a home or in a social situation, except in the most Westernised families. Never accompany your husband to a business meeting; Middle Eastern Arab men cannot discuss business in front of women.

All social occasions are for men only unless otherwise stated – and this is rare.

Westerners are often appalled by cruelty to animals in the Middle East. Dogs and donkeys are particularly badly treated and in Turkey I once saw the driver of a bus deliberately veer to the other side of the road to plough through a farmer's flock of geese. Despite the provocation it is a mistake to intervene on an animal's behalf; foreigners have been beaten up even for remonstrating. I know of a European who punched an Arab for maltreating a dog; he was lucky to escape with his life.

Bismi'llah means 'in the name of God'. An Arab uses this phrase whenever he does anything, hears of anything or tells anything, though he may use *Allahu akbar* (God is great) or *al-hamdu li-'llah* (Praise be to God). All references to the future, in hope or expectation, contain the expression *In sha'a 'llah*, or colloquially *Inshallah* (If God wills). A taxi-driver will often say *Inshallah* to a passenger giving him a destination.

The most usual exclamation in response to something exciting or surprising is *Wa'llah* (By God). God comes into many daily expressions, not only in praise, thanks and expectation but in condemnation, such as 'God curse your ancestors.'

BIBLIOGRAPHY AND REFERENCES

The following books are quoted from or referred to in the text. Each reference is numbered according to the sequence shown here.

1. Arberry, A.J., *The Koran Interpreted* (London: Oxford University Press, 1955) or *The Koran*, a translation by N.J. Dawood (London: Penguin, 1956)
2. Maqsud, C., *Crisis of the Arab Left* (Beirut: 1960)
3. Gibb, H.A.R., *Whither Islam* (London: Gollancz, 1932)
4. Hamady, S., *Temperament and Character of the Arabs* (New York: Twayne Publishers, 1960)
5. al-Hussayni, I.M., *The Crisis in Arab Thought* (Beirut: Dar Bairut, 1954)
6. Coon, C.S., *The Story of the Middle East* (New York: Henry Holt, 1951)
7. Khaldun, I., *The Muqaddimah – An Introduction to History* (London: Routledge & Kegan Paul, 1967)
8. Polk, W.R., *The Arab World* (Cambridge, Mass.: Harvard University Press, 1980)
9. Betts, R.B., *Christians in the Arab East* (London: SPCK, 1978)
10. Grunebaum, G.E., *Islam. Essays on the Nature and Culture of a Cultural Tradition*, (Wisconsin: Menasha, 1955)
11. Berger, M., *The Arab World Today* (New York: Doubleday Anchor, 1964)
12. Khadduri, M., 'The Role of the Military in Middle East Politics,' *American Political Science Review* (Washington, 1953)
13. Ammar, H., *Growing Up in an Egyptian Village* (London: Routledge & Kegan Paul, 1954)
14. Hussein, T., *An Egyptian Childhood*, (London: Routledge, 1932)
15. Dornier, P., 'La politesse bedouine,' (Paris, 1952)
16. Gibb, H.A.R., *Arabic Literature: An Introduction* (Oxford: Clarendon Press, 1963)

17. Malik, C., 'The Near East: The Search for Truth' *Foreign Affairs* (Washington, January 1952)
18. Lippman, T.W., *Understanding Islam* (New York: New American Library, 1982)
19. *Sayings of the Ayatollah Khomeini* (New York: Bantam Books, 1979)
20. *Qur'an [Koran] – Basic Teachings* (Leicester: The Islamic Foundation, 1979)
21. Hourani, A., 'Arabic Culture: Its Background and Today's Crisis,' *Perspective of the Arab World, an Atlantic Monthly Supplement* (New York: October 1956)
22. Lawrence, T.E., *Seven Pillars of Wisdom* (London: Cape, 1934)
23. Patai, R., *The Arab Mind* (New York: Charles Scribner's Sons, 1973)
24. Hocking, W.E., *The Spirit of World Politics* (New York: The Macmillan Co., 1932)
25. al-Jundi D., *Arab Nationalism in Modern Arab Literature* (Cairo: 1962)
26. Waddy, C., *The Muslim Mind* (London: Longman, 1976)
27. Derrick, J., *Africa's Slaves Today* (London: George Allen & Unwin, 1975)
28. Ali, A. Y., *The Holy Qu'ran: Text, Translation and Commentary* (Leicester: The Islamic Foundation, 1975)
29. Turki, F., 'To be a Palestinian,' *Journal of Palestinian Studies*, Vol III, No. 3, (1974)
30. Uwaya, S., in his academic paper, sent to the author
31. Antonius, S., in an article in the *Journal of Palestinian Studies*, Vol 8, No. 3, 1979
32. Young, I., *The Private Life of Islam* (London: Allen Lane, 1974)

Other Middle East books by John Laffin

Middle East Journey
Fedayeen – The Arab-Israeli Dilemma
The Dagger of Islam
The PLO Connections
The Arab Mind
The Israeli Mind
The Arabs as Master Slavers
The Arab Armies of the Middle East Wars 1948 – 1973
The Israeli Army in the Middle East Wars 1948 – 1973